THE PRESIDENT FOR LIFE PANDEMIC IN AFRICA

Kenya, Zimbabwe, Nigeria, Zambia and Malawi

Published by

Adonis & Abbey Publishers Ltd

United Kingdom
Southbank House
Black Prince Road
London
SE1 7SJ
United Kingdom
Emails: editor@adonis-abbey.com,
Tel: 0845 388 7248

Nigeria
No.3 Akanu Ibiam Street,
Aso-villa, Asokoro.
P.O. Box 10546
Abuja
Tel: +234 (0) 8165970458, 07066997765

Year of Publication 2013

British Library Cataloguing-in-Publication Data
A catalogue record for this book is available from the British Library

ISBN: 978-1-909112-31-5

THE PRESIDENT FOR LIFE PANDEMIC IN AFRICA

Kenya, Zimbabwe, Nigeria, Zambia and Malawi

Edited by

BHEKITHEMBA RICHARD MNGOMEZULU

Adonis & Abbey
Publishers Ltd

THE PRESIDENT FOR LIFE PANDEMIC IN AFRICA

TABLE OF CONTENTS

INTRODUCTION: A DIVERSE CONTINENT UNITED BY PRACTICES

Chapter 1: Broad Overview

COUNTRY CASE STUDIES

Chapter 2: Kenya

Chapter 3: Zimbabwe

Mugabe: Reinvention and Political Survival in Zimbabwe............63

Chapter 4: Nigeria

The Perpetuation of the Long Stay in Office by Nigerian Political Leaders..81

Chapter 5: Zambia

Frederick Chiluba's tactics used to sustain his stay in power..105

Chapter 6: Malawi

The president for life phenomenon: It all began here...............123

OVERALL CONCLUSION: GAMBLING WITH THE CONTINENT'S FUTURE..145

Acknowledgements

This book is a product of an intense study which started in 2008 when I was lecturing at Cape Peninsula University of Technology (CPUT). It was triggered by my very keen interest in political developments in Africa. I first published my initial ideas in the *Journal of Business and Management Dynamics (JBMD)* in December 2008. I would like to thank Prof. M. S. Bayat, then Editor-in-Chief of the journal and Dean of the Faculty of Business at CPUT for inviting me to submit my article. I would also like to thank Prof. Andre Slabbert, then Head of the faculty Research Department at CPUT. He always availed himself whenever I wanted to bounce my ideas and he gave me invaluable feedback on this and other research projects.

My sincere thanks and gratitude go to Mrs. Qondi Gumede (*uMaKhoza*) and Mr. Njabulo A. Gumede from Mtubatuba in Northern KwaZulu-Natal. I had an eye infection while writing this book. They hosted me and Mrs. Gumede typed up the information I either dictated to her or asked her to copy from my written notes-doing this free of charge. I cannot put in words my appreciation of their support. May God bless them!

I would also like to thank Mr. Marshall T. Maposa and Mr. Louis O. Akpan from the University of KwaZulu-Natal (UKZN), Edgewood campus, for agreeing to write chapters to be included in this book. Their country-specific insightful knowledge about the theme of this book was very useful. Mr. Maposa and I used to co-present academic papers on a wide range of topics on African politics and I was impressed by his cogent analysis of issues and his open-minded approach to discussions, not to mention his useful technical skills.

Prof. Murthee Maistry, then Head of School at Edgewood, demonstrated unmatched collegiality to me. He allowed me to use a laptop assigned to me when I was working with him even though I was no longer there as his Deputy and Senior Lecturer at UKZN. This left an indelible mark in my mind. Prof. Ufo Uzodike, Dean and Head of School of Social Sciences at UKZN remained my inspiration as I put this book together. He also agreed to write its foreword. I continue to respect his leadership prowess and foresight.

Last but not least, I would like to thank my beloved wife, Mrs. Jabu Silindile Mngomezulu (uMaMkhumane) and my family who sacrificed by allowing me time off to focus on writing this book instead of spending quality time with them. Words cannot express my appreciation of their understanding and support. In particular, I would like to thank my mom, Mrs. Nondlala Filda Mngomezulu and my dear sister Ms. Mavis Fanisile Mngomezulu. Their prayers and their confidence in me are the reason why I managed to finish this project. Mr. Joel Mafuleka, my religious mentor, will always be my pillar of strength-both on religious and social issues. The technical assistance of Ms. Leeann Govender from Durban University of Technology (DUT) is also much appreciated. To these and all those people whose names I could not mention here due to lack of space, may the blessings of God Almighty fall upon them!

DR BR Mngomezulu
January 2013
Durban

LIST OF MAPS

ABBREVIATIONS

ABN - Association for Better Nigeria (Nigeria)
AD - Alliance for Democracy (Nigeria)
AFORD - Alliance for Democracy (Malawi)
ANC - African National Congress (South Africa)
APP - All People's Party (Nigeria)
AU - African Union
CAF - Central African Federation (Central Africa)
CDC - Constitutional Drafting Committee (Nigeria)
COSATU - Congress of South African Trade Unions (South Africa)
DPP - Democratic Progressive Party (Malawi)
DRC - Democratic Republic of Congo (DRC)
EAC - East African Community (East Africa)
ESAP - Economic Structural Adjustment Programme
FDD - Forum for Democracy and Development (Zambia)
FRELIMO - Front for the Liberation of Mozambique (Mozambique)
GNPP - Great Nigerian people's Party (Nigeria)
GNU - Government of National Unity
GPA - Global Political Agreements
IMF - International Monetary Fund
KADU - Kenya African Democratic Union (Kenya)
KANU - Kenya African National Union (Kenya)
LCHP - Low Cost Housing Policy (Nigeria)
MCP - Malawi Congress Party (Malawi)
MDC - Movement for Democratic Change (Zimbabwe)
MMD - Movement for Multiparty Democracy (Zambia)
MPLA - Popular Movement for the Liberation of Angola (Angola)
MYP - Malawi Young Pioneers (Malawi)
NAC - Nyasaland African Congress (Malawi)
NARC - National Rainbow Coalition (Kenya)
NATO - North Atlantic Treaty Organization
NEC - National Electoral Commission
NECON - National Electoral Commission of Nigeria (Nigeria)
NEE - National Economic Energy (Nigeria)
NPN - National Party of Nigeria (Nigeria)
NPP - Nigerian People's Party (Nigeria)
NRC - National Republican Convention (Nigeria)
NTC - National Transitional Council (Libya)

OAU - Organization of African Unity
PDP - People's Democratic Party (Nigeria)
PRC - Provisional Ruling Council (Nigeria)
PRP - People's Redemption Party (Nigeria)
RENAMO - Mozambique National Resistance Movement
            (Mozambique)
SADC - Southern African Development Community (Southern Africa)
SAP - Structural Adjustment Programme
SDP - Social Democratic Party (Nigeria)
TANU - Tanganyika African National Union (Tanzania)
UDF - United Democratic Front (Malawi)
UN - United Nations
UNIP - United National Independence Party (Zambia)
UNITA - National Union for the Total Independence of Angola
            (Angola)
UPN - Unity Party of Nigeria (Nigeria)
UPND - United Party for National Development (Zambia)
WMDs - Weapons of Mass Destruction
ZANC - Zambian African National Congress (Zambia)
ZANLA - Zimbabwe African Nationalist Army (Zimbabwe)
ZCTU - Zambia Congress of Trade Unions (Zambia)
ZNLWVA - Zimbabwe National Liberation War Veterans Association
            (Zimbabwe)
ZANU - Zimbabwe African National Union (Zimbabwe)
ZAPU - Zimbabwe African People's Union (Zimbabwe)
ZUM - Zimbabwe Unity Movement (Zimbabwe)

FOREWORD

The position of "Dictator" was a highly respected title given in the Roman Republic (509-27 BC) to an "extraordinary magistrate" (*magistratus extraordinarius*). The job was a publicly-sanctioned responsibility. The incumbent dictator enjoyed unqualified authority to execute tasks that transcended the routine authority given to the "ordinary magistrate" (*magistratus ordinarius*). Indeed, dictators such as Julius Caesar assumed (on appointment) the authority not only of the chief executive but also of the supreme commander of the military forces of the Roman Republic. All other officials were subjected immediately to his full and unquestioned authority. Except for the Tribune of the Plebs, the ordinary magistrates and all other officials were subjected to the directives of the Dictator whose orders they were required to follow regardless of the circumstances. Those who dared to question or refuse to abide by the Dictator's orders risked the loss of their position and authority.

Without real peers, the dictator of the Roman Republic enjoyed not only unparalleled autonomy from the Senate but also extensive powers to dole out punishment without the inconvenience of a trial by the people. The Dictator's sentence had the value of the final judgment since there was no room to appeal it; the only recourse is to pray that he has a change of mind. And, of course, he enjoyed complete immunity from both the direct and collateral damages associated with his actions. The dictator of the Roman Republic had legal rights and powers not only to rule by decree but also to change any Roman law at whim and as he saw fit. In fact, he had the authority to even amend the Roman constitution without bothering with the necessity of ratification by the Roman assembly.

Clearly, dictatorships-both the legal or illegal variants-are not new to national and global politics; they were certainly not necessarily African inventions. Although Roman dictatorates would seem absurd in the 21st century to many who adhere to contemporary principles of democracy, the human impulse to move in that direction appears to be timeless. As events in Senegal demonstrated in 2012, the quest for control and power remains alive and transcendent of declared principles and logic. How else can one explain the decision by former President Abdulaye Wade-a well-known and respected critic of "sit-tight" governance arrangements-to rework Senegalese constitutional provisions to allow him a third and extended (seven-year) term as president? As with Julius Caesar -- who banned term limits and declared himself "Perpetual Dictator" in the Roman Republic -- and Napoleon Bonaparte of France who basically appointed himself "First Consul for life" in 1802, many contemporary leaders (in Africa and elsewhere) have a penchant for staying in power for as long as their citizens can tolerate - preferably as either a declared or undeclared "president-for-life". Where that fails, many are content to merely extend themselves by hook or crook in farcical election after farcical election. Some other rulers even extend themselves beyond their own death by forging systems that ensure they continue in office through their own descendants. A classic example is the ongoing attempt in North Korea to immortalize Kim Il-sung since his death in 1994. The leaders of his personality cult engineered a constitutional amendment that resulted in the permanent removal of the presidential office from the national constitution and the insertion of his name (constitutionally) as the "Eternal President". Subsequent North Korean heads of state are now reduced to "Supreme Leader" title.

Despite the wave of democratization that has seen major shifts in global politics and governance arrangements since the 1980s -- which seemed to culminate in 2011 in what initially appeared in North Africa to be tectonic movements away from sit-tight presidential terms-too many countries in Africa (and elsewhere) remain mired in non-democratic and mock-democratic governance arrangements that often betray malignant aspects of Roman Republican dictatorships. Over the years, it is that perception-albeit largely false-that has continued to inform and tarnish outsider opinions of African politics and African political leadership. As with Kwame Nkrumah (Ghana), Hastings Banda (Malawi), Jean-Bedel Bokassa (Central African Republic), Habib Bourguiba (Tunisia), and Idi Amin (Uganda), so with Muammar Gadhafi (Libya), Hosni Mubarak (Egypt), José Eduardo dos Santos (Angola), Teodoro Obiang Nguema Mbasogo (Equatorial Guinea), Robert Mugabe (Zimbabwe), Paul Biya (Cameroon), Yoweri Museveni (Uganda), etc.

After decades of political independence, there is now clear and growing evidence that most African leaders fail to distinguish themselves due not only to parochial pursuits but also to limited and unsustained vision about national imperatives and development. The net effect has been a legacy in many countries of: extensive poverty;

poor social and economic infrastructure; pervasive diseases; massive levels of unemployment; debilitating corruption and the associated dysfunctions; weakened authority structures, social bonds and values; and disarticulated bureaucratic, political, economic and social systems.

Of course, failing political and governance systems are fundamentally about failing leadership. Therefore, it is not surprising that an attendant feature of systemic ineffectiveness in delivering public services is negative citizen reactions, protests and demands aimed at their ruling elite. However, as the ruling class often are disinclined to give up the benefits and accoutrements of power despite the lack of capacity, vision or will to take the bold steps needed to transform the governance system effectively, they often respond by tightening their grip on power by not only undermining the civil liberties of fellow citizens but also by employing heavy-handed measures. Over time, as the controlling political leadership feels more threatened and vulnerable, they look to manipulate and circumvent constitutional strictures and formal political requirements. They may seek to ensure hassle-free life as former president by attempting to hand-pick a protégée as successor. Where the opposition is reasonably strong and able to mobilize adequate support, the damage imposed on the political system can be minimized. Where the opposition is mildly strong or disorganized, the government may attempt to use constitutional amendments and term extensions to stay in office. However, in countries where the opposition is weak and disorganized, the political leadership does not bother with manipulations. Instead, the will of the dominant political leadership is foisted with impunity on the citizenry with the modern day equivalent of Julius Caesar's "Perpetual Dictator" edict -- "President for Life".

Although new presidents often look to distinguish themselves as autonomous political actors, their ability to do so often depends on how well (and quickly) they are able to take control away from the personality cult of their predecessors. Obviously, the outcome of the struggle for power between the new president (and his following) and the hangers-on from the preceding regime often have immense implications for the nature and character of the new political dispensation within a country. It is this latter factor that makes this book an important contribution to our understanding of the African political landscape. In an environment with little or no institutional structures, legacy and memory, an individual or a small group can shape operational systems profoundly. Often, the net outcome of such political arrangement is the erosion of not only democratic principles and structures, but also of the rule of law, transparency, and accountability in governance.

It is for the above reasons that this book asks a crucial question: why are African leaders so reluctant to relinquish power? The document makes a determined effort to address this pertinent question. The broad overview presented in Chapter 1 provides the context within which this dysfunctional practice should be understood and interpreted. In this Chapter, Mngomezulu draws a distinction between the first and second generations of African leaders and argues that the second generation tends to cling to power for reasons different from those of the first generation. For instance, the latter remained in power for much longer partly because multi-party democracy had not been entrenched. Secondly, the African leaders who became the first presidents had led the struggle for liberation. Therefore, their stay in power was deemed a reward for their hard work.

The case studies of Kenya, Zimbabwe, Nigeria, Zambia and Malawi are used in the book to demonstrate how countries may descend into the abyss of bad leadership, succession politics, and the life presidency syndrome. Mngomezulu interrogates the actions of President Daniel arap Moi in Kenya and President Frederick Chiluba in Zambia to show how each sought to manipulate their way into longer presidential terms. Focusing on Nigeria, Akpan also shows how a range of Nigerian rulers manipulated and distorted the country into a deadly and dysfunctional political and social order by attempting to sustain and prolong their leadership positions. Maposa discusses the interesting and complex context of Zimbabwe where Mugabe (who became the country's first executive president in 1987) defies any attempt to box him within either the old or new generation of African leaders. Lastly, Mngomezulu and Maposa trace the concept of "president for life" to President Hastings Kamuzu Banda and Malawi where it was first used in Africa. They demonstrate how the concept played itself out in Malawi even long after President Banda was no longer in office.

The conclusion drawn in this book is that unless African political leaders transform their *modus operandi* on governance issues, the future of the African continent remains bleak. Mngomezulu argues that the onus is on African leaders themselves to revitalize the continent by emplacing more transparent and accountable systems of governance. As an incentive to encourage incumbent presidents to leave when their term of office expires and, hopefully, end the "president for life" pandemic, Mngomezulu proposes that former presidents should be given positions in appropriate structures such as the AU or UN so that they could feel valued and keep busy after leaving office.

In essence, this book takes the position that the future of Africa remains located in its leadership and governance arrangements. Africa's problems are rooted in the inability of African leadership to create and nurture effective governance systems capable of delivering essential services and development to their citizens in systematic and sustained ways. Therefore, the book envisions the need to devise a system that provides a soft landing to incumbent presidents by giving them a life line to continued relevance and influence after they stop being president. However, there is a proviso that for incumbent presidents to have a soft landing at the end of their tenure in office, they are obligated to avoid activities (illegal and immoral) while in office that may serve to turn their people against them. As the case studies in the book show, the key factor (besides financial benefits when one is at the helm) that shape the desire of sitting African presidents to make last-ditch attempts to retain power at all costs pertains to fear of prosecution or victimization after leaving office. Africa remains replete with enough examples of the "president for life" pandemic that its continuing relevance and saliency cannot be in doubt. This book makes a major contribution to our understanding and analysis of African political leadership and politics. In so doing, it provides invaluable lenses for assessing meaningfully the nature and role of African leadership in either retarding or fomenting development in countries throughout the region and the continent.

Prof. Ufo Okeke Uzodike
February 2013
Pietermaritzburg, South Africa

THE MAP OF AFRICA

Tunisia 1956

Western Sahara (disputed) U.N. Administered since 1991

Morocco 1956

Algeria 1962

Libya 1951

Egypt 1922

Senegal 1960

Gambia 1965

Guinea Bissau 1973

Mauritania 1960

Mali 1960

Niger 1960

Chad 1960

Sudan 1956

Eritrea 1993

Djibouti 1977

Guinea 1958

Côte d'Ivoire 1960

Sierra Leone 1961

Nigeria 1960

Central African Rep. 1960

Ethiopia Historically Independent

Somalia 1960

Liberia 1847 (Colony of repatriated Africans formerly held in American Slavery)

Upper Volta 1960

Togo 1960

Ghana 1957

Benin (Formerly Dahomey) 1960

Cameroon 1960

Democratic Republic of the Congo 1997 (Zaire - 1960)

Kenya 1963

Uganda 1962

Equarorial Guinea 1968

Gabon 1960

Rep. of the Gongo 1960

Tanzania 1964 (Tanganyika 1961)

Rwanda

Burundi 1962 1962

Angola 1975

Zambia 1963

Malawi 1964

African National Independence

Featuring the Dates of Independence of Each Nation

Namibia 1990

Zimbabwe 1979

Botswana 1966

Mozambique 1975

Madagascar 1960

Republic of South Africa 1931 (Apartheid ends 1994)

Swaziland 1967

Lesotho 1966

INTRODUCTION: A DIVERSE CONTINENT UNITED BY PRACTICES

Bhekithemba Richard Mngomezulu

Africa is a vast continent which covers a big landmass. Its more than fifty countries and smaller islands make it extremely difficult (if not impossible) for any historian or political scientist to assume that the continent is homogeneous. In fact, as Nugent (2004:1) suggests, "it is far more diverse than Europe." The prevalence of many ethnic groups within each country compounds this diversity even more, as do environmental differences. In Nigeria alone, as many as 250 ethnic groups exist. The East African countries of Kenya, Uganda and Tanzania also have no less than 200 ethnic groups apiece. There is also the lingering religious factor which continuously makes it difficult to assume that the continent, its regions and the different parts of each country are identical. The Islamic religion, for example, is not only dominant in North and West Africa, but also made inroads in East Africa from the times of pre-colonial trade and slavery. Noticeably, Islam, Christianity and indigenous religions compete for supremacy in each of the African countries and their regions. The North-South religious divide in countries such as Nigeria, Somalia and Sudan epitomize this conspicuously religiously-based bifurcation of the African countries.

Linked to the above is the issue of language. Not only do African countries differ in terms of their indigenous languages (which also differ within each country regionally), they also use different European languages depending on who colonized them during the Scramble for Africa. Consequently, former British colonies and protectorates have English either as one of their official languages or as the main language for conducting business and for admimistrative purposes. This is the case, in countries such as Ghana, Zambia, Zimbabwe, Kenya, Uganda, and the BLS states of Botswana Lesotho and Swaziland, to name but a few. Former French colonies in West Africa which include Cote d'Ivoire, Senegal, Togo and Mali use French as their linguafranca. Similarly, former Portuguese colonies such as Mozambique and Guinea-Bissau use Portuguese as their common language alongside other indigenous languages.

For those African countries that were once ruled or occupied by different colonial masters, their spoken foreign languages reflect this historical fact and reality. In Cameroon, for example, there is the French-speaking part and the English-speaking part of the country. Equatorial Guinea uses Spanish, Portuguese and French. In South Africa, English is one of the 11 official languages thus reflecting British influence. Afrikaans, which is close to Dutch, is another official language which serves as a remnant of Dutch occupation of the Cape of Good Hope. Trade and religion irrefutably created fertile ground for Arabic to infiltrate North Africa and is the official language in countries like-Algeria, Egypt, Libya, Morocco and Tunisia. We can thus deduce from these differentiating features that Africa is not only a vast continent but is also a heterogeneous continent in many aspects-. It should therefore be viewed and treated as such, and not as a single entity.

But having said that, it is worth noting that there are also certain factors that bind the continent together, some good and others bad. KiSwahili has managed to bring together countries such as Tanzania, Kenya, parts of Uganda, Eastern DRC, and parts of Rwanda, among others. This is something positive because Africans from these countries can communicate easily using a common language. From the bad side, one factor that is glaringly knitting the African continent together is the issue of African leaders who, once elected, or once they forcefully ascend to power, literally refuse or only grudgingly agree to leave office. As much as this practice is an antithesis of democracy, it is gradually gaining momentum. Gambia, Guinea and many others could be cited as examples. On the one hand, African leaders use brute force not only to ascend to power but also to retain it once they reach the top. In other instances, however, democratically elected presidents try to change national constitutions so that they could prolong their stay in office against the will of the people. This point is expounded in the book. While the former tactic is somewhat dwingling, the latter is gaining popularity and impetus.

Using a much bigger sample to expand on the latter submission would be too ambitious, if not completely foolhardy, although that would indeed shed more light on this pertinent topic. But for practical reasons, this book uses a manageable sample to demonstrate that the claim or submission made above has credence and can be authenticated. After presenting a broader context on this theme, an attempt is made to illustrate the point by using the case studies of five

African countries where leaders have successfully and unsuccessfully tried to elongate their stay in power beyond their mandate. These five countries are: Kenya, Zimbabwe, Nigeria, Zambia and Malawi. The various strategies used by different leaders in each country are enumerated and discussed to demonstrate the extent to which the 'president for life' mentality did not die with Malawi's founding President Hastings Kamuzu Banda. The latter ruled the country for over three decades but still refused to bow out and only did so half-heartedly when all his attempts to sustain his position had fallen by the way side.

CHAPTER 1

Broad Overview

Bhekithemba Richard Mngomezulu

1.1 Introduction and Background

The spate of unprecedented violence which engulfed a number of West and North African countries during the first few months of 2011 left the world numb, including members of the region themselves as well as the African Union (AU). Having to quell violence in more than one country at the same time came as a shock both to the AU and the international community at large. It also became difficult to focus on any one country while leaving others to battle it out on their own. This was a disturbing situation and a deplorable setback to the African continent. There were different speculations as to why this political violence broke out so suddenly and almost simultaneously. Some felt that it was the people of those countries genuinely looking for better solutions to their local problems so that they could improve their lives by removing their leaders whom they held responsible for their plight. Others unabashedly blamed the West for being behind all these violent activities in order to meet their own economic and political needs (Jagire, 2011; Mngomezulu, 2011; Campbell, 2011). Whatever the correct reasons were the fact that these violent activities happened at about the same time raised eyebrows, both locally and internationally.

It is surprising that having been loyal citizens for so many years, African communities suddenly turned against their leaders, forcing them to leave office almost immediately. This was never going to be easy because these leaders had been in office long enough to establish a working relationship with state institutions including the police and the army. They could revert to these state institutions and quell the rebellion. The Libyan case, for example, is a very fascinating one. For more than four decades since the 1967 coup it seemed as if things were in order, especially given that everyone knew that Colonel Muammar Gaddafi had been their leader for so long with very minimal opposition from a few of his fellow citizens. It was generally taken or believed - that his leadership was unquestionable. His decision to give oil money to ordinary Libyans won him the support of the majority of Libyans. Therefore the call that he should step down from office was a great surprise to all those who followed the turn of events with a keen interest since he assumed power at the tender age of 27. The thought of grooming his son and making him his protégé was a strategy for Gaddafi to continue ruling behind the scene if he were to leave office. This strategy failed. Obviously it was a foregone conclusion that a strategy like this one would not work under the prevailing circumstances because the masses had already made up their minds that they wanted a new leadership and begin a new political path. To a large degree, at a more general level the violent activities were unexpected-except, of course, in the Ivorian case which was almost inevitable to avoid such actions given the unstable political situation in that country after independence. But even leaders like Gaddafi and President Hosni Mubarak of Egypt knew all along that they were seating on a timed bomb which could explode at any time.

As for the rest of the unrests, even some local citizens were in shock when they broke out. Who would have ever thought that a political giant like President Mubarak would be challenged by his own people after ruling them for more than thirty years and ran what appeared to be a rather stable government? But once violent activities began in Egypt, it became quite clear to everyone that the nationals knew exactly what they wanted to achieve, that is, to remove their leaders from office - including Mubarak and set up a new regime. Nothing could stop them from this resolution which they were prepared to fight and die for if necessary. They therefore resolved to implement it no matter what and eventually, they succeeded in doing so.

In the entire Egyptian history the year February 2011 will go down either as the trigger of the democratization process in that country, or as the event which ended Mubarak's long rule. Whatever route these changes take henceforth, the reality is that the Egyptian history has already undergone considerable reconfiguration since the outbreak of the violence. The fall of Mubarak already has serious political repercussions, both locally and internationally and will continue to do so for many years to come. This includes an impact on the positive relations he had with other world leaders at a personal level and also through bilateral agreements signed between Egypt and other governments in Africa and abroad. Whatever the outcome of these developments, the events which culminated in the resignation of this giant leader in Africa who had kept the Arab League and other institutions running for many years have already found a place in

Egyptian history. Whether Mubarak will be remembered as a hero or a dictator is a decision Egyptians and other interested parties will continue to debate and make conclusions intuitively. One of the mistakes President Mubarak made was that of pushing for his son to succeed him (Mngomezulu, 2011). This created the impression that he saw Egypt as a monarch and this cost him dearly, politically speaking.

The political events highlighted above present themselves as some of the great events of the century in Africa. This can be discerned firstly in the manner and order in which they happened; and secondly, in the way in which the AU and the North Atlantic Treaty Organization (NATO) responded to the uprisings (especially those that broke out in Libya). Gaddafi was almost a god in Libya and no one would dare cross his path, the Western community included. When such a man was told to leave office the world seemed to be shocked by the news - except those who may have sponsored the rebel forces clandestinely.

But the fact that members of NATO immediately called for an attack on Libya without any negotiations, gave the impression that what happened is what they were waiting for so that they could use it as a pretext for ousting Gaddafi from office. This is not surprising because the same strategy was used by President George W. Bush of America against Saddam Hussein. He manufactured lies that President Hussein had Weapons of Mass Destruction (WMDs) so that he could get the support of other countries. Indeed countries like Britain and France never scrutinized nor questioned this; they just sent their troops to destroy Iraq. Something similar happened with Libya. Even when African political formations opposed this stance, they were literally ignored by Western countries such as America, Britain and France. The mere fact that NATO continued to bombard Libya against the AU's position that there had to be a ceasefire which would allow for negotiations to take place vindicate those who believe that the West somehow had something to do with these violent activities that took place in Libya. This also undermined the AU as a political body charged with the task of handling African affairs and also serves as a link between Africa and the international community, including both the United Nations which gave NATO permission to attack Libya.

This trajectory is given substance by the fact that as the violent activities continued there were already those who wanted to see Gaddafi dead. One wonders if this was not pre-meditated by certain countries which had issues with Libya as a country or Gaddafi as a leader long before the eruption of violence in his country. The mysterious assassination of the Chief of Staff of the rebels who was once Gaddafi's right-hand man provides substance to these speculations. This was the same strategy used by America to cause havoc in Iraq. Whether investigations will reveal the actual circumstances under which the Chief of Staff was assassinated remains unclear. But what seems clear at this stage is the fact that this assassination was carefully planned and meticulously executed in order to make a statement. The Chief of Staff may have been killed by government forces as alleged in the media. But, on the other hand, there is a great likelihood that NATO could have been behind the assassination so that they could stir emotions and thus strengthen their case for sustaining the NATO attacks on Libya.

The circumstances around the eventual death of Colonel Gaddafi leave a lot to ruminate about in retrospect. First, it is worth noting that there was no respect for International Law in NATO's activities in Libya. According to International Law, war prisoners are not killed once captured. They are apprehended and handed to the invading or defending country's authorities for trial at a later stage. But in the case of Libya, Colonel Gaddafi did not die in combat; he was captured alive by the invading forces. Thus, the most logical action according to International Law would have been for - NATO forces to apprehend and hand Colonel Gaddafi over to the International Court of Justice to face trial for the crimes he was alleged to have committed while - in power. Instead, the NATO forces summarily executed him by shooting him on the head. This was against International Law. Sadly, Secretary-General of the United Nations, Ban Ki Moon, took no action. In fact, he did not even deem it necessary to question the actions of NATO. Instead, he showed a sigh of relief that Colonel Gaddafi was dead and Libyans now had a chance to rebuild their country and put in place a democratic government that would be tasked to unite the country. As some would argue, this demonstrated lack of fair and objective leadership from the UN Secretary General.

The events that followed soon after Colonel Gaddafi's assassination buttress the views expressed above on procedural matters. When it was confirmed that Colonel Gaddafi had been killed, no arrangement - was made to have him buried within 24 hours as per the Islamic religious practice. Instead, his half-naked body was displayed as a trophy-head in Masrata for public viewing. Moreover, members of the public were even allowed to take pictures of the slain

Colonel Gaddafi using cameras and cellular phones with the sole purpose of mocking and ridiculing him. When he was eventually buried together with his son, he was whisked away during the early hours of the morning so that people would not see where he was being taken to. The National Transitional Council (NTC) did everything possible to hide his desert grave from the public. The four people who witnessed his burial had to first swear on the Koran that they would never reveal the location of the grave. Defending this decision, the National Transitional Council unabashedly argued that it wanted to prevent a situation whereby the grave could be made a shrine by those who still supported Colonel Gaddafi thereby presenting a potential for disunity in the country. This action showed beyond any doubt that the West-supported NTC was determined to completely erase Colonel Gaddafi's name from the history of Libya and create an environment where Libyans would start building their country on a new slate devoid of the vestiges of the old order. By so doing, the NTC also deprived the world of a significant aspect of Libyan history.

The events in Egypt and Libya discussed above serve as a stark reminder that Africa is cursed by leaders who want to die in office while doing literally nothing for the masses they lead, but only enrich themselves and those close to them. These leaders do not care how many of their citizens suffer or even die as a result of this obsession with political power. While some citizens die 'naturally' as a result of socio-economic conditions created by the incumbent leaders, others are gunned down for standing for their rights and for the truth. Therefore Gaddafi's statement to the media that he would either rule or kill his people should be understood in this context. Similarly, before tendering his resignation President Mubarak had been in power for thirty years and yet he still wanted to retain his position and prolong his stay in office. If this could not happen, he was prepared to groom his son to succeed him and eliminate those who stood on his way. How does one explain this? Are we still in the monarchy system where you groom your son to rule after you have left office? This and other niggling questions will surely remain with us for as long as we live. The manuscript will explain some of the reasons for this without providing conclusive answers. The aim is to trigger further research in this area which is pertinent to Africa.

Another question which begs attention in this regard is the following: What is it that Africa's long-time serving leaders still wanted to achieve which they could not accomplish during the many years in office? This question raises a serious concern about the reasoning of some of the African leaders who are definitely driven by egotism and political avarice to make unpopular decisions so that they remain in power. To make sure that such decisions are implemented by hook or by crook, they use bribery, persuasion as well as brute force and assassinations. By and large, these leaders push the politics of the belly and the needs of their families first before those of the masses who voted them into power. However, we should be brisk to mention that this is not only an African disease. Similar cases can be found in Eastern Europe and in other parts of the world where leaders become gods and want to remain in office indefinitely. Surely, this happens for different reasons from the ones found in different parts of the African continent. But the African situation is disappointing because instead of the problem dissipating somewhat as one would expect in a democratizing world, - it keeps gaining momentum. This is a serious concern and perhaps the reason why the masses have recently taken the decision to free themselves from their oppressive leaders they once revered. They call for their 'second independence' which would free them from their own people - the African leadership.

In a way, this is an endemic and deep-rooted problem in Africa which needs concerted efforts from all stakeholders to up-root. At independence in the 1960s and 1970s it became fashionable for the newly elected incumbents who had been leaders of political movements to run their countries as though they were monarchs or emperors (Cooper, 2002). However, the context was different. For example, the absence of opposition parties and the fact that to a large extent the masses approved of their long stay in office became the common excuse. Some used force to retain their positions. President Hastings Kamuzu Banda of Malawi spent 30 years in office but still wanted to extend his stay. Had there been no political revolution which culminated in Bakili Muluzi ascending to power, he would have managed to prolong his stay. President Banda even declared himself 'President for life'. The same story repeated itself in many parts of Africa. This was the case, for example, in Equatorial Guinea where President Teodoro Obiang Nguema Mbasogo assumed power on 3 August 1979 follofing a successful coup of his uncle dictator Francisco Macia Nguema in August of the same year and has been in office for over three decades. In the Congo too, Mobutu Sese Seko retained power after taking it from President Joseph Kasavubu. He kept his position until he was ousted by Laurent Kabila. In Zimbabwe the country's citizens know no other leader other than President Robert Mugabe who has been in office since that country obtained independence in 1980 (this point is expounded by Maposa's chapter in this manuscript). At his age (88), one would expect President Mugabe to leave office gracefully and enjoy his pension in peace. He could still provide advice to his successor should a need arise. But this is not in sight. He wants to hold power until his last day on earth. This is sad because he will not be remembered like people such as former President Nelson Mandela of South Africa. Instead, people will remember him as a ruthless and a power hungry dictator who refused to relinquish power even when he had lost the elections.

The question that needs to be posed at this juncture is the following: Why are these leaders so reluctant and, in fact, unwilling to leave office? Using five different case studies from the African continent, this is the question the present manuscript is wrestling with and to which it is trying to make a contribution. It does this by providing at least some of the reasons for certain actions taken by African leaders at different political moments. But before presenting these case studies it would be appropriate to provide the broad African context within which some of the actions mentioned above should be viewed and interpreted. The case studies will then augment and supplement this information by providing concrete examples from various countries as to how these events played themselves out in those countries.

1.2 The General Trend

Pre-colonial African states such as those of Ghana, Mali, Songhai, Great Zimbabwe and Buganda (to name but a few) thrived before the advent of colonialism in Africa (Njoh 2006; Hanson 2003; Young 2001; Hull 1976; Reader 1997). They did very well with no help from the East. This proved that Africans have the ability to survive on their own if they do things their own way instead of being forced to copy the procedures of other countries. It also debunks the myth that before colonialism Africa knew nothing about administration and overall governance; and that they only learnt this from their white counterparts. The end of colonial rule during the 1960s and 1970s brought optimism that the African masses would regain their dignity bestowed on them by their creator and taken away - by the greedy European countries. As the Western flags were lowered and replaced by the national flags of the African countries, -optimists were vindicated that indeed Africa was on a new course or was traveling on a new path which had a potential to move the countries to the stratosphere. This was a justifiable optimism. Sadly, not long thereafter the new black incumbent presidents became obsessed with power once they assumed leadership positions. Instead of dismantling colonial institutions and ending old practices, they protected and consolidated them for their own political gains. This meant that only the face changed from white to black but the countries remained the same or worse off.

Initially, the African masses were tolerant of these practices and rejoiced that their black leaders - most of whom had fought relentlessly against colonial rule - were now enjoying the luxury previously perceived to be the prerogative of white masters who ruled over them. In their view, this was a deserved reward to these leaders. However, as the black leaders settled in their new positions they did not dream of ever relinquishing power to any one, both black and white. This was a huge disappointment to the masses that had supported them all along and a huge blow to what was perceived to be a smooth transition from colonial rule to independence. As the latter mobilized to oust their once-revered leaders, unfortunately these incumbent presidents became even more ruthless and made indefatigable attempts to remain in office at all cost. This cast a pall on the African continent as a whole. The introduction of one-party states, the promotion of ethnicity and nepotism - coupled with maladministration and inexperience - triggered more political violence which led to bloodshed in many parts of Africa. In response, the incumbent leaders resorted to more brute force to address the situation and consolidate their positions. It is in this context that I ask the question: why did African leaders become so obsessed with power in this book. I hope that the book will shed some light on this and other questions even though it is impossible to provide conclusive answers to the many questions - surrounding this theme in African history and African politics.

From the discussion above and by doing a very quick survey of five African countries regarding this problem we can conclude that there are two types of presidents who have stayed in office almost indefinitely in Africa. The first group would be those who were seen by their masses in different African states as gods of some sort and whose continued stay in office was tolerated and generally perceived to be nothing but the reward for the suffering they went through and the dedication they showed towards the liberation struggle. Their holding the office for a longer period was seen as a fair compensation for the troubles they endured. Presidents such as Julius Nyerere of Tanzania and Kenneth Kaunda of Zambia falls in this category. There are then those like Robert Mugabe who were also part of this group but soon got drunk with power once they were in office and used brute force and other strategies to sustain themselves (Mngomezulu, 2008: 36-48). After creating enemies, it became difficult for them to leave office fearing that once they lost political power they could be prosecuted by their successors. These points are further developed below to provide the necessary context needed in order to understand what some African leaders have done and (in some instances) continue to do in order to remain in power - much longer.

1.3 The First Generation of African Leaders

The independence of the Gold Coast in 1957 marked a watershed in the history of - African continent. During this year, the colony of the Gold Coast was re-named Ghana with Kwame Nkrumah at the helm. African leaders derived inspiration from this episode and pressed for their own political independence from European oppressors. Consequently, a number of African countries rid themselves of colonial rule in the early to mid-1960s. In East Africa, Tanganyika African National Union (TANU) took a vanguard position in this regard by leading Tanganyika into self-rule in 1960 and full independence a year later, which was then confirmed in June 1963. Uganda followed suit in 1962, and then Kenya and Zanzibar in 1963. In 1964 Tanganyika and Zanzibar merged to form Tanzania as the country is known today. Other countries like Angola and Mozambique gained their independence in the mid-1970s. Zimbabwe joined the party in 1980 under Robert Mugabe who did not look suspicious at the time. The independence of these and many other African countries marked a new epoch in African history in that, for the first time since the scramble for Africa began in 1885 as a result of the Berlin Conference of 1884-1885, Africans ruled fellow Africans. This looked fair and proper for Africa while the Europeans were not happy to leave their comfortable seats.

But 'presidents' for life - possibly the most odious coinage of African independence - entrenched the rule of the newly elected presidents who competed with traditional rulers for power and treated them as colonial stooges and relics of a conservative past (Russell, 1999; Cooper, 2002). This view is premised on the fact that some of Africa's first generation of leaders who took over from colonial rulers set a wrong precedent by holding onto power as though they were monarchs. In 1958, Dr. Hastings Kamuzu Banda returned to Malawi after spending 40 years abroad and working as a doctor in Ghana. He led the Nyasaland African Congress (NAC), which was banned in 1959 and Banda was imprisoned only to be released the following year. When he came out of jail in 1960 he led the Malawi Congress Party (MCP) on whose ticket he became prime minister in 1964. With the adoption of the republican constitution in 1966, Banda became Malawi's first black president and "in 1971 this was altered to president for life" (Wiseman, 1991:25). President Banda ensured that most of the government portfolios were entrusted to him and his office. Even when he became too old to rule, he still refused to relinquish power. This set a wrong precedent, hence the conclusion that Banda was "Africa's first but sadly not last president for life" (Russell, 1999: 41). Other African leaders continue to replicate this abhorrent practice and for some reason they seem to enjoy the way it works although it upsets the masses within Africa and the international community in general.

The fact that the leaders who emerged as presidents had been leaders of the liberation struggle against colonial rule came with different sets of problems. Firstly, those who had been with them in the bush envied their success and became critical of how they were running the newly independent countries. At times they did not even give them the respect they deserved as Heads of States. Secondly, some of the masses revered their new leaders and tolerated their actions even if such actions were not good. For them, it was justifiable that these first presidents should remain in power for much longer because after all they were the ones who had led the struggle to oust colonial administrators and therefore had to be rewarded for their hard efforts. It was in this context that Kenyans referred to their first president, Jomo Kenyatta, as *Baba wa Taifa* (a Kiswahili phrase meaning 'Father of the nation') (Archer 1969:131). Each of these scenarios is expounded below with the aim of contextualising the analysis.

1.3.1 Opposition to the Incumbent President

It is a truism that when African leaders embarked upon the liberation struggle against colonial rule they did not agree on the strategies they would use to accelerate the pace of getting rid of the colonialist (Sowetan, 2007). Consequently, there was more than one liberation movement in each country which claimed to represent the wishes of the masses. For example, Kenya once had the Kenya African National Union (KANU) dominated by the Kikuyu ethnic group, and the Kenya African Democratic Union (KADU), which drew support mainly from other ethnic groups but more particularly the Luo ethnic group from western Kenya. Mozambique had the Mozambique National Resistance Movement (RENAMO) and the Front for the Liberation of Mozambique (FRELIMO), while Zimbabwe had the Zimbabwe African National Union (ZANU) and the Zimbabwe African People's Union (ZAPU). In South Africa, although the African National Congress (ANC) had remained the only liberation movement since 1912, in 1959 the Pan Africanist Congress (PAC) was formed by a group of disgruntled ANC members who had divergent views from the party's majority on the inclusion of non-blacks in the liberation movement. They argued that the ANC was for black people only and when this view was not accepted by the organization they decided to move out and establish theirs which would only have blacks as members. That is how the PAC came into existence

When independence was achieved in many of these African countries, leaders of various liberation movements saw themselves as the custodians of the newly independent states. Those who failed to realize this dream made life difficult for the new incumbents. On many occasionsthe latter returned to the bush and started waging a new war against their former comrades-in arms. This culminated in a number of the first coups experienced in - Africa. This was the case for example in countries such as Zaire or Congo Republic (1961), Ghana (1966) and Nigeria (1966). There were also failed coups in countries like Tanzania (1964) and about two decades later, in Kenya (1982) and in Zambia (1988). Even in South Africa where democracy only came in 1994, inter-and intra-party conflicts claimed the lives of thousands of people in what was commonly but wrongly dubbed 'black on black violence'. When the ANC-led Government of National Unity (GNU) was formed, conservative Afrikaners formed the Boeremag and planned to topple the government and reinstate white rule in the country but this failed.

Other African countries witnessed prolonged civil wars. This was the case in Angola where Jonas Savimbi, leader of the National Union for the Total Independence of Angola (UNITA) dedicated his whole life to the fight against the Popular Movement for the Liberation of Angola (MPLA) until his death on 22 February, 2002. Mozambique and the Democratic Republic of Congo (DRC) went through a similar experience and the results were disastrous. In Zimbabwe, Joshua Nkomo challenged Mugabe. The fall-out between the two resulted in the ruthless killing of about 20,000 people from Matabeleland (Nkomo's support base) by a predominantly Shona military force. Subsequently the Senate of Edinburgh University recently revoked an honorary degree awarded by the university to Mugabe in 1984, arguing that it was not aware of these atrocities committed by Mugabe's army when it conferred the degree on him (Pretoria News, 2007). To a large extent, all these developments unwittingly contributed to the 'president for life' phenomenon. Mugabe became even more ruthless to his people in a bid to show Britain that he was in charge of Zimbabwe and there was nothing they could do aboutit. This has continued unabated to-date. Mending the relationship between Zimbabwe and Britain is not in sight.

Incumbent presidents devised ways and means of consolidating their positions. On the one hand they became more dictatorial and crushed any opposition ruthlessly as Mugabe did. This was also the case in the Republic of Congo where Prime Minister Patrice Lumumba was brutally assassinated in 1961 simply because he was a critic of the incumbent president, Joseph Kasavubu. In Uganda, when Milton Obote felt that his position was under threat from the Kabaka of the Buganda Kingdom he waged war against him in 1966. The latter claimed the autonomy of his kingdom, arguing that it was legitimized by the Buganda Agreement of 1900, which he signed with the British (Low, 1971, Mngomezulu, 2004). Idi Amin Dada was even more ruthless when he took over power after ousting President Obote in 1971. By the time he left office following a successful invasion from Tanzania in 1979, he had allegedly killed about 300, 000 people (Wiseman 1991: 5). Idi Amin had a habit of awarding himself preposterous and pompous titles, such that he was viewed as 'a figure of fun abroad' (Wiseman, 1991: 14). However, there was nothing amusing about his rule for the people of Uganda, both black and

Indian. In fact, it is believed that he will go down in history as "one of the most vilified mass murderers of the twentieth century" (Bater, 2005: 8). This is how far African leaders were prepared to go in order to retain power.

Some of these leaders went for a softer option in their bid to remain in office. They declared their countries one-party states to prevent political opposition. This was a subtle form of defusing the opposition in order to prolong their stay in office. As discussed later in this manuscript, KANU remained the only party in Kenya for several years before multiparty democracy was adopted in 1992. Even the most popular African leaders once toyed with this idea and, in fact, implemented it at some point. In 1965, President Nyerere made TANU the only party operating in Tanzania. Zambian president Kenneth Kaunda declared the United National Independence Party (UNIP) the only permitted party in 1972. Sometimes these actions instigated even more violent reaction from the belligerents, as was the case in Kenya in 1982. All these tactics were geared primarily towards entrenching the position of the incumbent president who felt threatened by the opposition but was not ready to hand over power to the new claimants.

Looking at things from this vantage point, we could confidently conclude that the reason why the incumbent presidents wanted to remain in office forever was that they had a strong belief that the offices they occupied were a reward for their relentless and successful struggle to free their nations from colonial oppression. They were determined to enjoy what their white predecessors had enjoyed for decades while they were still in the bush. It was in this context that when they assumed power they imported expensive cars, clothes, furniture and food to match their elevated social status (Cooper, 2002; Mazrui, 1986; Davidson, 1984). By all accounts, it was not easy for them to relinquish power and live a normal life again, which is why they did all they could to remain in office for life. Driven by their own political avarice and financial reasons, those with whom they had fought against the colonialists also wanted to reap these fruits of freedom because they had equally suffered for the country. Unfortunately, those already in power felt that the cake was too small to be shared. They therefore resolved to preserve their positions at all costs.

1.3.2 Support for the Incumbent President

Another reason why the first generation of African leaders remained in office almost indefinitely was because they enjoyed the support of the masses whom they had led to independence. It was due in part to this reason that a leader like President Kaunda was able to rule Zambia for almost three decades. As one author puts it: "the Zambian leader was, however one of the few genuinely likeable Big Men" (Russell, 1999: 55). He was seen as "a popular democratic leader who was dedicated only to the uplifting of the Zambian people without undue concern for his own position" (Wiseman, 1991: 105). Although corruption flourished under President Kaunda's rule, he remained untainted by it and this consolidated his popularity with the masses. In East Africa, President Nyerere was perceived as a leader about whom it was difficult to have harsh opinion. He was seen as "the most meaningful and significant leader ever produced in Africa" (Van Rensburg, 1981: 392). In the case of Zimbabwe, during his early years in office Mugabe could do no wrong among his supporters. So, "when the first cases of corruption and incompetence came to light, they were excused: after all, this was the man who had ended long years of white rule" (Russell, 1999: 292-293). Although this changed a few years later, Zimbabweans revered Mugabe and his administration during the early days of the country's independence.

Sometimes African leaders were more skilful in their *modus operandi*. They delivered on certain promises and argued that the longer they remained in power the more they would be able to address the needs of the people they were leading. This made the masses believe that their leaders were driven by empathy and altruism to remain in office, not by political greed. One author captured this meticulously cogitated tactic elegantly with regard to President Nyerere. He recalled: "At the time of Tanganyika's independence in 1961, Nyerere used to say to friends, 'if only I can have three years', 'if I can have just five years" (Smith, 1973: 201). Indeed, after returning from his voluntary resignation in 1976, President Nyerere remained in office until 1985. Even during the 1965 elections after the merger of Tanganyika and Zanzibar in April 1964 to form Tanzania, he remained the most popular leader among his people. His popularity was such that "the party was not prepared to nominate anyone to oppose him, in all likelihood no one would have chosen to run against him anyway" (Smith, 1973: 151). He was the darling.

President Nyerere was enjoying the fruits of his labour. He had embarked upon the struggle to free his people when he returned from pursuing his studies in Europe. In 1955 he appeared before the United Nations. It was the first time an African had been sent by a territorial political organization, in this case TANU, to represent his people's hopes to the UN (Melady, 1961). It was in this context that when he passed away in 1999 some commentators stated that his death deprived independent Africa of one of its most intelligent, perceptive and determinedly radical leader. He was described as "an inspiration not just to Africans but also to people all over the world" (*New Internationalist,* 1999). Despite the failure of his socio-economic policies like *ujamaa,* President Nyerere remained one of the most popular African leaders in Africa even after his demise.

It follows from this discussion that some African leaders did not necessarily force themselves onto the people they were leading. Instead, they were loved by them and were perceived as messiahs. A similar situation occurred in Swaziland where the monarch, King Sobhuza II ruled the tiny kingdom from 1968 until his death in 1982. The Entrenchment of democracy was not an issue in Swaziland at the time. With a few exceptions, people generally accepted that it was preordained who their leader would be and therefore they did not mind being ruled by him indefinitely as per custom. That is why it is still so difficult to promote democracy in Swaziland till to-date. On 5 September, 2010, the Congress of South African Trade Unions (COSATU) and twenty-one countries around the globe demonstrated against King Mswati III for silencing opposition and not allowing freedom of speech in Swaziland. It was acceptable for monarchs to remain in office indefinitely because custom allowed it. But presidents, unlike monarchs, cannot remain in office forever because their positions are created by democratic principles, not their birth into primordial families. In short, the first generation of African leaders remained in office mainly for two reasons:

(i) They used force to remain in power;
(ii) They derived support from the people they were leading. In both instances they were either perceived, or perceived themselves as the right people to lead their countries because they had been at the vanguard of the liberation struggle for many years. Either way, the president for life phenomenon prevailed.

It would therefore be safe at this point to argue that political allegiance and fear of victimization by incumbent leaders have seen African masses allowing their leaders to become presidents for life. By and large, challenging such leaders became tantamount to digging one's own grave at broad daylight. But once the masses decide to act, they do so decisively and put their lives on the line as discussed in the cases of Egypt, Libya and Ivory Coast.

Using five countries as case studies, this manuscript demonstrates vividly how the two types of practices have managed to keep presidents in office even when it was crystal clear that they had become dispensable as political leaders. Each of these cases presents an empirical account of how the president for life phenomenon played itself out and under what circumstances. General and inside accounts are used to paint a broader picture about the turn of events. In the end, the book shows how African leaders managed to sustain themselves for such long periods of time in office without the masses turning against them until recently.

1.4. Conclusion

It is clear from this broad overview chapter that Africa has gone a long way to be where it is today. But what is also evident is the fact that some of its leaders ascended to power under false pretence. They stated that their primary aim was to oust Europeans and let Africans run their affairs. As soon as they came to power they, for the first time, tasted Western derived luxury. They occupied beautiful houses and used offices once used by their predecessors. From the bush they suddenly lived a lavish lifestyle and became gods almost overnight. This made them have second thoughts about the promises they had made to the masses when they were still leaders of the liberation struggle. This was a bad omen and did not augur well for the future life of the general populace. It meant that the revolution only culminated in the change of face from white to black but not the methods used to rule the people. It was, at least in part, due to this reason that in some countries fellow freedom fighters returned to the bush and started to wage war against their former comrade-in-arms. This has remained regrettable and one of the dark sides of the African past. Such a practice has continued to tarnish the image of the African continent.

But, as discussed above, a confluence of factors (both endogenous and exogenous) played an instrumental role in letting the first generation of African leaders after independence sustain their stay in office. Among others were: the populace's thinking that these leaders deserved to hold leadership position much longer because this was a reward for their efforts to oust colonial rulers; the financial and material support some received from their former masters; the force they used to impose themselves on the masses; weak opposition; the treacherous and perfidious manner in which they won potential detractors through bribery, to name but a few. Through these and other tactics, the new political leaders were able to elongate their stay in power.

The advent of democracy in the 1990s marked a new epoch in African history. Some African leaders who had ruled their countries under the old order thought that they could still operate within the constitutional framework to prolong their stay in power. They tried this by proposing constitutional amendments that would allow them to run for the office of presidency beyond the time that was agreed upon when such constitutions were drafted. This time they failed. The five case studies discussed in this manuscript demonstrated how such plans were scuttled by opposition parties as well as some members of the incumbent president's ruling party. The book is organized in such a way that it will make an easy read, since each chapter, except for chapter 1, tackles- one country.

Chapter 1 is a broad overview in which I provide the wider context for the rest of the discussion in the manuscript should be understood. I divide the 'presidents for life' into two categories: the first generation and the second generation. I then discussed various reasons why leaders from each category wanted to elongate their stay in power. This approach debunks the general assumption that African leaders are just one homogenous group. Already in this Chapter, I give snapshots of the developments that took place in various countries across - African continent, including the five case studies discussed in detail in this manuscript in subsequent chapters. This prepares the reader's mind-set on what to expect in the following chapters.

Chapter 2 is the first of the five case studies discussed in the book. In this Chapter I use the case study of Kenya to show in vivid and explicit terms the different ways in which Presidents Jomo Kenyatta and Daniel arap Moi either portrayed themselves to the electorate or tried to force themselves onto the masses and thus prolonged their stay in power. The chronological succession politics of Kenya from 1963 to 2002 in this Chapter is presented in order to assist those readers who are not well versed with African history in general and Kenyan history in particular.

Chapter 3 focuses on Zimbabwe. In this Chapter, Maphosa eloquently takes a closer look at Mugabe's manoeuvres which have kept him in power for more than three decades despite rampant opposition to his rule in recent years. Maphosa traces Mugabe's tricks from the days of guerrilla warfare which ended Ian Smith's rule, to the time when he was a credible nationalist leader (a statesman of note), and when he literary became a heartless monster. Most importantly, Maphosa ends the chapter by looking at Mugabe as a post-colonial pugilist. In literary terms, Maphosa presents Mugabe as a round character, someone who demonstrates different features at different moments. In the end, Mugabe becomes a friend, an enemy, a patriot, a dictator and a unifier.

Chapter 4 is about Nigeria. Akpan looks at the eventful history of Nigeria from the time of independence in 1960 to the time when President Olusegun Obasanjo left office. He addresses the short-lived independence and civilian administration and spends time on the endless coups and counter coups that have come to characterize Nigeria in both African and global politics. Moreover, Akpan does an analysis of the policies these leaders successfully or vainly tried to implement at different political moments. Lastly, he takes a look at how President Obasanjo left office. Akpan raises questions about the egocentric decisions taken by President Obasanjo when he realized that he was leaving office and discusses the impact of bad leadership in Nigeria on the well-being of the people in education and other spheres of life.

Chapter 5 is a case study of Zambia. In this Chapter I begin by tracing the history of the country way back to the 10th century. I discussed how the geographical space which is called 'Zambia' today was settled by earlier African communities. I then spent time discussing various reasons why President Kenneth Kaunda (affectionately known as cde KK) was able to rule Zambia for almost three decades. Following on this is succession politics after his departure from office when he was beaten by Frederick Chiluba, a unionist. The selfish nature and extravagance of President Chiluba is exposed in this chapter. His corrupt practices also came to fore through the charges levelled against him by a British court which acted on the request of Zambia's Attorney-General. Although lootocracy seems to be a common feature in African politics, I specifically showed how it worked in the case of Zambia. Also key in the discussion are the methods used by Chiluba to keep Kaunda out of a possible come-back in Zambian politics - a strategy which worked for him and will go down as one of his very few successes while in political office.

Chapter 6 has a specific focus on Malawi. Here, Maphosa and I begin the chapter by presenting the geographical location of this country and its population. We then briefly but chronologically discussed the country's colonial experience till independence. The thrust of the discussion is on the country's political and succession history. The roles played by President Hastings Kamuzu Banda and President Bakili Muluzi get special attention as both leaders showed signs of being obsessed with power regardless of how such power benefited the people they ruled. The actions of President Bingu wa Mutharika are also discussed very briefly in this Chapter to demonstrate change and continuity evident in his leadership style. These discussions show how each leader pushed the idea of elongating his stay in office, mainly for his own financial and political gains, not for the masses.

A general conclusion of the book then follows. Its aim is basically to try and pull the strands together and show how these five narratives are different from and/or similar to one another.

Secondly, in the conclusion, I discuss what the future holds for the African continent if its leaders continuously push their personal agendas at the expense of the people who voted them into positions of power. I reiterate the point that the five case studies used in the manuscript do not in any way suggest that these are the only African countries where the 'president for life' phenomenon can be found. Instead, the five countries are used to demonstrate both the nature and extent of the problem. Lastly, I suggest direction for further research on the theme tackled in this book, paying attention to the fact that the president for life pandemic continues to cause a dent to the image of the African continent. Importantly, I suggest possible solutions to this scourge so that - African continent could regain its prestige in the international scene.

References

Archer, J. (1969). *African Firebrand: Kenyatta of Kenya*. New York: Julian Messner.

Bater, J. (2005). *Heroes and Villains*. New York: Thomson Gale.

Campbell, H. (2011). "Libya must not be partitioned", in *Contemporary Africa Review*, Issue No. 14, April: 8-11.

Cooper, F. (2002). *Africa since Independence: The Past of the Present*. Cambridge: Cambridge University Press.

'Call to rehabilitate Zulu Prince' published in *Sowetan*, 31 May 2007.

'Chiluba guilty of stealing £23m from Zambia' published in *Pretoria News*, 5 May 2007.

Davidson, B. (1984). *Africa: The Story of A Continent* (Video series). Chicago: RM Arts.

Hanson, H. E. (2003). *Landed Obligation: The Practice of Power in Buganda*. Portsmouth: Heinemann.

Hull, R. W. (1976). *African Cities and Towns before the European Conquest*. New York and London: W. W. Norton & Company.

Jagire, J. (2011). "Why Gaddafi's overthrow may be bloody", in Contemporary Africa Review, Issue No.14 April: 14-15.

Low, D. A. (1971). *The Mind of Buganda: Documents of the Modern History of an African Kingdom*. London, Ibadan and Nairobi: Heinemann.

Mazrui, A. A. (1986). *The Africans: A triple heritage* (Video series). Washington DC and London: WETA and BBC.

Melady, T. P. (1961). *Profiles of African Leaders*. New York: The MacMillan Co.

Mngomezulu, B. R. (2004). "A political history of higher education in East Africa: The rise and fall of the University of East Africa, 1937-1970. Unpublished PhD Thesis, Rice University.

Mngomezulu, B. R. (2008). "Leadership crisis in Africa: Contextualising African leaders' obsession with power", in *Journal of Business Management Dynamics*, Vol.2 Decembe:36-48.

Mngomezulu, B. R. (2011). "The Egyptian crisis and the president for life pandemic in Africa", *Contemporary Africa Review*, Issue No.14 April:27-28.

Njoh, A. J. (2006). *Tradition, Culture and Development in Africa*. Burlington: Ashgate.

Reader, J. (1997). *Africa. A Biography of the Continent*. England: Penguin Books.

Russell, A. (1999). *Big men, little people: The leaders who defined Africa*. New York: New York University Press.

Smith, W. E. (1973). *Nyerere of Tanzania*. London: Victor Gollancz.

'The Lion Lies Down. Julius Nyerere comes to the end of an anti-colonial life', *New Internationalist*, Issue 319, December 1999.

Van Rensburg, A. P. (1981). *Africa's Men of Destiny*. Bloemfontein: De Jager-Haum.

Wiseman, J. A. (1991). *Political Leaders in Black Africa: A Biographical Dictionary of the Major Politicians since Independence*. England: Edward Elgar.

Young, C. (2001). "Nationalism and ethnic conflict in Africa," in M. Guibernau and J. Hutchinson (eds.), *Understanding Nationalism*. Cambridge: Polity Press.

COUNTRY CASE STUDIES

CHAPTER 2: KENYA

Playing the Ethnicity Card: Presidents Kenyatta and Arap Moi

Bhekithemba Richard Mngomezulu

THE MAP OF KENYA

2.1 Introduction

The history of Kenya has deep roots which different African and Africanist scholars have tried to trace using archaeological evidence, oral history and linguistics. Through these mechanisms, the histories of various ethnic groups have been documented. The colonial and postcolonial periods have been recorded using colonial records stored at the Kenya National Archives (KNA) in Nairobi (Kenya) and the Colonial Archives in Britain, to name but a few.

The purpose of this chapter is to briefly trace the history of Kenya from the pre-colonial times, discuss the colonial era which began in 1895 followed by the coming of the British settlers, and spend time discussing succession politics following the withdrawal of Britain from this country in 1963. The protagonists in this narrative are Presidents Jomo Kenyatta who came from the Kikuyu ethnic group and Daniel arap Moi who was a Kalenjin from the Rift Valley. One of the major themes addressed in this chapter is ethnicity. An attempt is made to demonstrate how ethnicity shaped Kenyan politics after independence, both during the reign of Kenyatta from 1963 to 1978 and during the reign of Moi from 1978 until 2002. Lastly, the role played by ethnicity in the ascendance of President Mwai Kibaki to power is given attention. However, the theme of the manuscript (the president for life phenomenon) is discussed with specific reference to the first two presidents, that is, Kenyatta and Moi. President Kibaki is not factored into the equation. This decision is informed by the fact that as this manuscript is being finalised, preparations are already underway in Kenya for the next Presidential elections and the incumbent president is not one of the contenders, nor has he tried to emulate President Moi in trying to elongate his stay in power.

2.2 A Brief History of Kenya

Contrary to the general practice whereby the historiographies of African countries tend to begin when an African country was already in the process of being colonized by a European country, the reality is that the history of Africa did not start with colonization. Similarly, the history of Kenya did not in any way begin from 1895 when the British came to settle in the highlands of the geographical space we now know as Kenya. The history of this area has deep roots which go back as far as before 1500. In fact, an interpretation of fossils recently found in

East Africa, indicates that, protohumans inhabited this area more than 20 million years ago. Findings near Lake Turkana in Kenya show that hominids lived in the area about 2.6 million years back. Cushitic-speaking people from north- Africa then settled in the area now known as Kenya around 200 BC. Arabs started arriving in the coastal area of Kenya from about the first century AD and by the 8th century both Arabs and Persians built settlements there. Subsequently, in the millennium AD Nilotic and Bantu people arrived. The interaction between the Arabs and the Bantu culminated in the formation of the Swahili language which was used as a lingua franca for trade purposes.The British only came into the picture during the nineteenth century, 1895 to be precise (Iliffe, 1995; http://africanhistory.about.co m/od/Kenya/p/KenyaHist.htm).

It therefore came as a surprise that Bruce Berman, a political scientist and John Lonsdale, one of the most renowned historians began their introduction in *Book One* of *Unhappy Valley* by saying the following:

> Once upon a time a smart set lived in Kenya's Happy Valley, at the foot of the Nyandara Mountains. Immigrant clan of British aristocracy, they were good at handling guns, women and a constant flow of champagne. Some of them seasonal refugees from northern winters, their playground had been carved by the colonial state from the dry season pasturage of the former lords of East Africa, the Maasai (Berman and Lonsdale, 1992:1).

Whether these authors were quoting James Fox or simply decided to start Kenyan history from this period remains unclear. But whatever the reason for their action is, it was inconceivable that they would forget to prefix this quotation with a few lines in which they stated their views or position on the pre-colonial history of Kenya, which should be the starting point. They would then look at what predecessor scholars have done when writing about Africa in general and Kenya in particular. Alternatively, they could have made a disclaimer on the issue of the origins of the Kenyan peoples. Their failure to do this left them vulnerable to scathing criticism by other scholars. The fact that the sub-title of the book is: *Conflict in Kenya and Africa* makes the need for a historical background even more appropriate and expedient. Reading the first page of the introduction to *Unhappy Valley*, one is left with the thinking that the two authors subscribe to the obsolete myth that Europeans came to Africa to redeem Africans and make them 'good' people, whatever such a phrase meant in real terms. This observation is given substance when the two authors present the view that: "Drugs, drink and dalliance had perhaps made the natives lose their respect" (Berman and Lonsdale, 1992:1). Inferred here is that the natives once had respect.

According to this trajectory the British had the responsibility to resurrect the natives from the ashes and make them real people again. This is a shallow way of thinking, especially if one considers the fact that evidence abounds that civilization started in Africa, not in Europe as others would want us to believe. Among the resourceful sources in this regard is Giday's (1992) relevant but also provocative title *Ethiopian Civilization* which vividly demonstrates how the Ethiopian civilization developed at different moments. As discussed above, in the case of Kenya and other parts of East Africa archaeological evidence shows beyond doubt that all human beings originated from this region. Obviously this history predates colonialism. It is therefore safe to say that African history in general, and Kenyan history in particular, has deep roots which pre-date colonialism. This is an irrefutable historical fact.

What is clear with regards to the history of Kenya is that by the time the British arrived in the region in 1895, each of the ethnic groups or, should we say societies, already had sound and rich histories. Ehret (2001), talks about two of Kenya's earliest societies whichpopulated the Eastern Highlands. These are the Gumba and the Thagiicu. Both societies lived long before 1500. It would be unthinkable that these and other societies in Kenya would wait until Europeans showed up to be innovative and live their lives to the fullest like their counterparts in other parts of the world.

But what is worth mentioning at this juncture is that there was no unity among Kenyans at the time as we know them today. In fact, even the name Kenya had not been coined yet. People developed themselves as local and ethnic communities. Therefore we had for example: the Luo/Jaluo/Joluo, Kikuyu/Gikuyu, Kalenjin, Mijikenda, Kamba, Maasai, Gusii, Nilotes and many such groupings. People used these groupings to identify themselves when a need arose. Each of them had its own way of interacting with nature, teaching its youth, inculcating values to the youth, providing cure for different diseases and basically surviving in a hostile environment (Iliffe, 1987) with an unbelievable level of intelligence and innovation. For years, histories with Western inclinations were blatantly silent about local histories until Kenyan historians such as the copious and world renowned Professor of history Bethwel Ogot, the late Atieno Odhiambo, William Ochieng' and many others from the East African region took a conscious decision and initiative to bring these histories to the fore so that people could read them (Ogot, 2009; Ogot, 2002; Ogot, 1999a; Ogot 1999b; Ogot, 1982; Ogot, 1976; Ogot, 1968; Ogot, 1967; Cohen and Odhiambo, 2004; Odhiambo, 2001; Cohen and Odhiambo, 1992; Odhiambo, 1989; Ochieng', 1987; Ochieng', 1986; Ochieng', 1979; Ochieng', 1975; Ochieng', 1974).

One may argue that these were simply local ethnic histories and therefore did not in any way cover wide ground for them to attract a diversified and broader audience. To be sure this criticism would be hard to totally refute because there is an element of truth in it. For example, Odhiambo (2001) wrote specifically about the Nilotes. Ogot (1967) wrote about the history of the southern Luo and Ochieng' (1986) wrote about the Gusii. However, it would also be erroneous to accept this criticism in its entirety and unequivocally. It is through such efforts of writing local histories that we, at least, have a glimpse of Kenya before colonialism. The nationalist histories only followed a few years later in line with the spirit of nationalism and independence. There is vast literature in this regard produced by both African and Africanist scholars globally.

In the context of East African territories of Uganda, Tanganyika and Kenya, the latter (Kenya) was naturally better positioned compared to the rest of the territories. Geographically it was located in the highlands and therefore the coolest of the three geographical spaces. For that reason Kenya became a settler colony. This would have a long-lasting effect a few years later when the colony came of age and started to make strides in terms of serving the mother-country, Britain or becoming semi-autonomous. By comparison, the settler population in Kenya was very high compared to territories like Uganda which was a British protectorate but with a significant number of Africans who lived there compared to whites. Tanganyika too was not attractive to the settler community except for a few Germans at some point when they controlled the territory. Thus, Kenya became the darling of the British. But constitutional changes were not accelerated in such a way that they could promote social harmony among different racial groups. The colonial government in Kenya and the central government in Britain did not always see things the same way on certain matters. This is reflected in the parliamentary debates in both the House of Commons and the House of Lords where the colonies and other issues were discussed (Mngomezulu, 2004).

But having said all that, I would be remiss not to mention that Kenya's geographical advantage made her a rallying point in East Africa's economic and political life. When regional bodies such as the East African Community (EAC) were established (1967-1977), most of the Headquarters of the Community's institutions were located in Nairobi, Kenya. This forced Uganda and Tanganyika to complain, a move which culminated in the relocation of certain Headquarters to either Uganda or Tanganyika. The fact that Kenya was the last of the three East African countries to obtain independence in 1963 following Tanganyika in 1961 and Uganda in 1962 could be seen as Britain's attempt to hold on to power for a little longer in Kenya. But because of the pressure exerted mainly by Tanganyika under President Nyerere the British were forced to bring the date of Kenya's independence a little bit closer so that the region could move forward together in order to prevent possible competition and unequal readiness in future when they had to join hands in establishing a federation. President Nyerere was the number one supporter of the view that his country (Tanzania), Uganda and Kenya had to form a federation (Low, 1971; Mngomezulu, 2004; Mngomezulu, 2006).

Thus far, we have interrogated unfounded perceptions about Africans and their histories and also paid particular attention to Kenya in a bid to see how she fits into the broader scheme of things. The focus of this chapter will now shift to succession politics in Kenya from independence with the founding nationalist leader, President Kenyatta at the helm in 1963 to the unceremonious departure from office of President Moi in 2002 and the ascension of President Kibaki to power. Such a discussion is necessary not only in terms of presenting the chronological political history of Kenya since independence (important as that might be) but also to show how each of these leaders (especially the first two presidents) played the ethnicity card to elongate their stay in office.

2.3 Succession Politics in Kenya

The Mau Mau uprising of 1952 to 1956 (some authors argue that the dates are October 1952 to December 1959) is credited for ending colonial rule in Kenya. This is hard to refute. Although the uprising was eventually suppressed by the colonial authorities, it, indeed, paved the way to freedom. Jomo Kenyatta who had been incarcerated by the British for his role in the fight for liberation came out of jail to lead a highly charged Kenyan citizenry as Prime Minister and, later, as the country's first President under the new political dispensation. So, when Kenya became independent in 1963 Jomo Kenyatta became the President. He remained in this position until he died of natural causes in State House Mombasa on the coastline on 23 August 1978. At this point, Daniel arap Moi who had been vice-president since 1967 immediately assumed office, first in an acting capacity, then as a duly elected president of the country as per the nation Constitution. For the next 24 years Moi ruled Kenya, first as a harmless politician but, later, as a ruthless ethnic chauvinist who had no regard for the life of the next person. This blatant persecution of Kenyans, especially those from the Luo and Kikuyu ethnic groups whom he viewed as contenders to his position, only ended in 2002. This landmark incident was made possible by the coming together of 14 opposition political parties to establish the National Rainbow Coalition (NARC).

But why did it have to come to this in the first place? How could one person rule a country for 24 years and still refuse to leave office when his constitutional mandate came to an end? Obviously there are different explanations for this action. But these can be summarized into three causal factors: the rigging of the elections, the use of force and intimidation as well as allegiance and reverence shown by his close confidantes. As far as Moi was concerned the time he had already spent in office was not enough for him to satisfy his thirst for power. He wanted to prolong his stay in office a little longer so that he could continue enjoying the privileges which accompanied the position of being president. Even the manner in which he eventually conceded defeat and handed power over to Kibaki showed clear signs of an angry man who still had a sore heart and only grudgingly relinquished power because he had run out of options. The question which begs attention is the following: How did Presidents Kenyatta and Moi manage to remain in office for so many years? A related question could be phrased as follows: What made it difficult for them to hand over power to other leaders? These questions will be the focus of this section.

2.3.1 Jomo Kenyatta

President Kenyatta falls under the category of the first generation of African leaders. These were nationalist leaders about whom the masses were patient because they had been at the forefront of the liberation struggle for many years. In the case of Kenya the masses called President Kenyatta *Baba wa Taifa*, a KiSwahili phrase meaning 'Father of the Nation'. Others referred to him as *Mzee*, literally meaning 'an old wise man'. The majority of Kenyans could not see any other leader who qualified to lead Kenya besides President Kenyatta. For that reason they did not mind him remaining in office almost indefinitely.

But despite this almost certain support, President Kenyatta still had to be strategic when doing certain things so that he created the impression that he was still the darling of Kenyans and a unifier. His popular KiSwahili phrase '*harambee*' [let us pull together] was part and parcel of this agenda. He created the impression that if Kenyans worked together a bit harder, they would most certainly is in a better position to take the country forward. Secondly, there were instances when President Kenyatta played the ethnicity card. In the main, his cabinet was dominated by his fellow Kikuyu kinsmen. To appease the Luo who seemed to be a potential threat to his power, President Kenyatta appointed Jaramogi Oginga Odinga as his Deputy-President. This move was well received by the Luo community who reside in the Kisumu area in Western Kenya. For the time being President Kenyatta managed to keep the nation together.

However, the reality in East Africa in general and in Kenya in particular is that politics in this geographical space revolves mainly around ethnicity (Cohen, 1974). President Kenyatta was acutely aware of this reality. When things suited him he won the hearts of the Luos by appointing one of their own as Vice-President. When he realized that Vice-President Odinga was gaining support which might threaten his position in future, he ridiculed him in public and this did not go down well with the Luo. This incident brought ethnic politics back in the limelight and instigated clashes which left a number of Kenyans dead and some critically injured. President Kenyatta became sceptical about the Luo. Moreover, Odinga was an unapologetic communist while President Kenyatta had capitalist inclinations. This aggravated an already volatile political situation. In the light of the above, President Kenyatta then looked for a candidate with a low profile, someone he thought would not mobilize against him at a later stage. That is how Moi, a Kalenjin, became vice-president in President Kenyatta's cabinet in 1967.

Moi was not perceived as a potential threat to both Kikuyu and Luo powerbrokers. The Kikuyu, in particular, "broadly welcomed his succession to the presidency assuming he would be a pliant leader who would do their bidding" (Russell, 1999:72). In a nutshell, President Kenyatta used a combination of strategies to remain in office. These included political fame, the fact that he was an old man and when the going got tough he inevitably reverted to the ethnicity card to mobilize Kikuyu support while ostracising the Luo. Had he not died of natural causes in 1978, all signs show that President Kenyatta would have remained in office for much longer than the time he spent in power as long as the Constitution was silent on how many years he could serve as the country's president. His death thus robbed him of this opportunity to prolong his rule. He inadvertently handed it over to Daniel arap Moi who used his own tactics to sustain himself in his position for the next 24 years. Moi even labelled himself 'the Professor of politics' because when people thought he was out he always found a way to save his political career. But how did he do that? We address this question in the next sub-section.

2.3.2 Daniel Arap Moi

In a way, the assumptions by the Kikuyu and Luo about Moi proved to be correct, at least for the first few years of Moi's presidency. In the main, Moi was a tactician who knew when to act and how. He strategically dubbed his era as the *nyayo* (footsteps) period. This created the impression that he would carry on with President Kenyatta's legacy and follow on his footsteps in terms of policy formulation and implementation. To gain the support of the Kikuyu on this he continued to rule Kenya using the same team he had inherited from his predecessor, President Kenyatta. Even his minor cabinet reshuffle, which the national constitution allowed him to do, did not in any way demonstrate a significant change of direction of his government. President Moi tactfully retained Charles Njonjo, an influential Kikuyu political giant in his cabinet as Attorney-General. Moreover, he strategically appointed Mwai Kibaki, another Kikuyu, as his Vice-president. All these signs demonstrated that Kenya was indeed going through a very smooth political transition under the leadership of President Moi (Van Rensburg, 1981; Mngomezulu, 2008).

As reality would have it, there was no way President Moi would keep things smooth for a long time. As discussed earlier in this chapter, ethnicity plays a key role in the history of the East African region, which includes Kenya. Moi was a Kalenjin and had learnt from Kenyatta how to play the ethnicity card to one's advantage. As mentioned above, keeping the Kikuyu contingent in the cabinet was a way of buying time while finding his grip on power. The opportunity for him to act presented itself in a rather awkward manner. It was the 1982 attempted coup by the air force which gave Moi a reason to invoke his ruthlessness. After crushing the attempted coup which was dominated mainly by the Luo and leaving dead bodies outside Kenya's Broadcasting House, he then turned to the Kikuyu. One by one he pushed them to the political wilderness. This included Charles Njonjo the Attorney-General whom he kicked out of the cabinet in 1983, soon after the incident mentioned above. This ethnic war continued unabated for the remainder of the 1980s such that by the early 1990s "Moi was ringed by a coterie of Kalenjins, many of whom were country peasants trying to get in on every deal, the bigger the better, even when they had no idea of commerce" (Russell, 1999:73).

During this time, a new crop of influential politicians came from the Kalenjin, not the Kikuyu. The list of Moi's confidantes included politicians such as Nicholas Biwott, Mark Too and many others, all of whom were Kalenjin from the Rift Valley, President Moi's place of birth. Once Moi was sure about the support of those he had surrounded himself with, he then put his plans into action. Vocal politicians who were determined to expose Moi and challenge him on certain political issues disappeared mysteriously. They were either never found or were found dead. This was the case, for example, in 1990 with John Robert Ouko, one of the vocal and smart Luo politicians who served as the minister of Foreign Affairs at the time. Hon. Minister Ouko had a serious argument with Moi on a particular issue after which he left for his hometown in Kisumu. Somehow, on his way back from home he never reached Nairobi. He simply disappeared in thin air. Everything was done to cover up the fact that he was assassinated by state security agents under the instruction of the highest-ranking state officials who were sent by Moi. A murder docket was opened. But as the case continued in court, some of the witnesses to the case simply disappeared in thin air. Others were found dead but the perpetrators were never apprehended and brought to book. This instilled in the minds of Kenyans the fact that anyone who crossed his path did so at his or her peril. In that way Moi could do as he pleased and elongate his stay in office.

In political terms the death of Hon. Minister Ouko soon after quarrelling with Moi remains one of the many scars in Moi's presidency. The Minister's family had great hopes that since he was a smart man with sharp brains Moi would tap into his wisdom and bring him closer to himself. But the fact that Hon. Minister Ouko was a Luo was enough to leave President Moi convinced the he could not be trusted and therefore deserved to die. Indeed, this incident robbed Kenya of one of her sharp brains. Two fellow Luos, David William Cohen and the late Elisha Stephen Atieno-Odhiambo subsequently published a well-researched and point blank book about Minister Ouko's death. The book by the two authors raises very critical questions about this incident about Moi's leadership in general (Cohen & Odhiambo, 2004; see also Rake, 2001).

Many other politicians across the ethnic divide, including Raila Odinga, son of Oginga Odinga, faced the wrath of President Moi's security agents who wanted to make a name for themselves so that they could be liked and trusted by him and hopefully benefit from his political manoeuvring. Interestingly, the majority of these atrocities were committed at Nyayo House in central Nairobi although other politicians faced their fate in other places around the country. One wonders if this was still the footsteps Moi had promised when he assumed office as president. From the humble politician that he portrayed himself to be in the mid-1960s, President Moi became a feared monster as he gradually found his grip on power. He became untouchable. This sustained him in office, not because he was loved anymore, but because he was feared by the masses and small opposition parties together with their leaders.

It is fair to argue that actually President Moi got drunk with power and used heinous tactics to demonstrate it to the public. But the fact that ethnicity is such a determining factor in East African politics means that any other leader would have been tempted to invoke it whenever a need arose. However, the difference with President Moi is that unlike President Kenyatta who only showed his awareness of what ethnicity could do for him and used it in his favour, President Moi used ethnicity to spill the blood of his fellow Kenyans - a regrettable act. For this reason, history will judge him as someone whose leadership was tainted with blood.

Of interest for our discussion is the fact that President Moi continuously portrayed himself as a law-abiding politician. In this context, as much as he wanted to stay in office indefinitely, he planned to do so within the confines of the law. Thus, when he realized that his term of office was about to end he remembered how he had wronged a number of Kenyans from ethnic groups other than his, the Kalenjin. He meditated about what would become of him once he was no longer the president of the country and therefore not protected by the Constitution from prosecution. Given these thoughts, he immediately carved a plan to rescue himself. He went to parliament with a proposal that there should be an amendment of the national Constitution so that it would allow the president (himself) an opportunity to run for the presidency for the third time. This was a way of buying time so that he would then use his third term in office to plan for his exit accordingly. Had this tactic succeeded, he would have managed to remain in office for much longer without being accused of doing so against the wishes of the electorate.

But because President Moi had already annoyed many people (both politicians and civilians), he stood no chance of making his plan sail through in parliament. In fact, what he failed to realize was the fact that there had been a proliferation of political parties in Kenya by this time. These small parties knew that none of them could win against KANU which was an old political party, let alone against a sitting president. Therefore they vowed to put their differences aside and speak in one voice in order to scuttle Moi's ploy. In the end, a total of fourteen political parties came together to form NARC. As the day of the election drew closer, the writing was already on the wall that Moi's tried and tested political manoeuvring had become obsolete and had run out of steam to be able to withstand the tornado that was coming his way. Not even his trusted secret agents could stop this 'wind of change'. As expected, Uhuru Kenyatta, the candidate Moi had subsequently hand-picked to represent KANU lost the elections.

It should be noted that Moi's political miscalculations left him exposed. He assumed that by 2002 he still had the venom he once possessed at the apogee of his political career. It never struck his mind that he would be forced to leave office in such a disgraceful and unceremonious manner as the fourteen small political parties put their efforts together. The popular song which dominated the rallies and, later, the inauguration of Mwai Kibaki as new president was '*yote yawezekana bila Moi*' [everything is possible without Moi]. This song left him convinced that he was not wanted anymore to continue to rule Kenya and that the small political parties had the full backing of the electorate who had voted against KANU in the recently concluded election. After all, when he had the power to do so, he somehow abused it. Moreover, he directly or indirectly orchastrated the death of many vocal Kenyan politicians, mainly those who came from ethnic groups other than his own, the Kalenjin.

Ethnic politics played an instrumental role in ending Moi's rule. After his plan to continue the Kalenjin 'kingship' was thwarted, he strategically identified Uhuru Kenyatta, the son of President Kenyatta to succeed him and made him his protégé. The aim behind this decision was to appease the Kikuyu whom he had persecuted for various reasons over the past few years. He now planned to leave them with the idea that he had no hatred against them but trusted their son as the potential leader who could best fit his shoes when he left office. Had he done this prior to trying to have the Constitution amended perhaps the situation might have been different. By all accounts it was too late to start thinking about the Kikuyu now that he had run out of options. All in all, he was just preparing himself for a soft landing but was not thinking for the Kikuyu. Some were quick to notice this. As a back-up, Moi also tried to win the Luhya ethnic group. In order to appease this group, the out-going President Moi appointed Musalia Mudavadi as his Vice-president. Interestingly, Mudavadi never attended even a single parliamentary session. KANU lost the elections and a new government was constituted without Mudavadi who had even lost his seat in his hometown. Even if he had won the constituency seat and Uhuru Kenyatta won the presidential elections, there was no guarantee that Mudavadi would have retained his new position as Deputy President. In fact, Moi counted on the fact that Uhuru Kenyatta was his protégé and would therefore not disappoint him. However, given that a number of Kikuyu politicians had suffered in the hands of Moi while in office, there were great chances that such politicians would have influenced Uhuru to sing a different tune after winning the elections.

The build-up to the 2002 elections was a fascinating moment in Kenyan history. There were back-to-back rallies at Uhuru Park and Nyayo Stadium addressed by KANU and NARC leadership respectively. In all the rallies I attended, the ethnicity card was an ace card. NARC realized that a candidate from other political formations linked to small ethnic groups stood no chance of winning against the Kikuyu which formed the majority in KANU. Consequently, they settled for Mwai Kibaki, a Kikuyu, in order to divide the Kikuyu vote and still enjoy the support of the rest of the smaller ethnic groups. By the time President Moi realized what was happening around him, it was too late to carve another plan since the day of the elections was around the corner. He therefore conceded defeat, and so did Uhuru Kenyatta. NARC registered a landslide victory and Mwai Kibaki emerged victorious. Despite his serious injuries sustained in a mysterious car accident during the political campaigns, Kibaki was flown back from Britain to assume the reigns as Kenya's third president since 1963. The inauguration ceremony held at Uhuru Park was ecstatic. The jovial mood confirmed that Kenyans were relieved to see President Moi vacating office at long last. He also could not hide his disappointment, which is why he did not even attend the state lunch prepared at State House Nairobi for the newly crowned president and other dignitaries. Instead of mingling with the Heads of States (or their representative) he had worked with, he briskly flew to his farm in Baraka Estate to begin his retirement.

Soon after Kibaki's inauguration as Kenya's new president, concerns were raised about the 'Mount Kenya Mafia'. This was in reference to the dominance of Kibaki's 'homeboys' in his new cabinet, which was seen as a continuation of Moi's practice of surrounding himself with his 'homeboys'. Both real and perceived favouritism practices were reported in the media. But it should be noted that although President Kibaki also played the ethnicity card, he did not use it to sustain his stay in power. This marked a deviation from Moi. However, he ran for office for the second term despite his earlier promise that he would only serve for one term. Anyway, he still operated within the confines of the constitution.

2.4 Conclusion

This chapter has traced the history of Kenya, starting from the pre-colonial times when the British had not yet arrived in the region to lay - claims and exercise their influence. By so doing, the chapter has implicitly challenged the general practice whereby most African histories tend to start from the colonial period and ignore what Africans used to do as societies long before the advent of colonialism and imperialism, both of which cogently and literally destroyed the entire African fabric. Consequently, not enough is known today about pre-colonial African societies and their innovative ideas which enabled them to inhabit and tame the African hostile environment. By discussing the different stages the history of Kenya went through over many years and providing examples to give substance to the arguments made, the chapter presented and portrayed Kenya as a country on the move.

Most importantly, this chapter has demonstrated in the case of Kenya how President Kenyatta, the founding president, and President Moi, his successor, both promoted the notorious 'president for life' syndrome. The chapter demonstrated that ethnicity, imprisonment, political assassination and many other factors came handy in assisting the two politicians achieve their ultimate goal of elongating their stay in power. However, the chapter also demonstrated that no matter how strong, intimidating, cruel and ruthless a leader might be, the electorate and small opposition parties can oust such a leader if they stop operating as separate entities but join hands and face the incumbent leader as a strong and formidable unit. This assumption is given credence by a detailed discussion of the strategy used by NARC in its bid to oust the self-acclaimed 'professor of politics' (President Moi). When the latter tactic is used, not even the ethnicity card can save the incumbent leader. President Moi hand-picked Uhuru Kenyatta as his successor so that he could appease the Kikuyu he had persecuted during his long stay in office. Moreover, he appointed Musalia Mudavadi as his Vice-president in an attempt to calm down the Luhya ethnic group and win their support should his successor decide to prosecute him. But, as seen above, none of these strategies worked for him. In the end, he had to grudgingly concede defeat and bow out of office.

As shown in this chapter, President Moi will go down in history as one of the African presidents who got drunk with power and wanted to die in office against the wishes of the people. But he was not the only one to do so. Africa is replete with examples of leaders like him, people who wanted to remain in office almost indefinitely. The next chapter will address the 'president for life' phenomenon from the Zimbabwean point of view. An attempt will be made to show how President Robert Mugabe has succeeded to prolong his stay in power besides playing the ethnicity card which seems to have dominated Kenyan politics since independence.

References

Berman, B. & Lonsdale, J. (1992). *Unhappy Valley*. Oxford: James Currey. Nairobi: E. A. E. P., Athens: Ohio University Press.

Cohen, D. (1974). *Urban Ethnicity*. London: Harper & Row.

Cohen, D. W. and E. S. Atieno Odhiambo. (2004). *The Risks of Knowledge: Investigations into The Death of Hon. Minister John Robert Ouko in Kenya, 1990*. UK: Ohio University Press.

Cohen, D. W. and E. S. Atieno Odhiambo. (1992). *Burying SM: The Politics of Knowledge and the Sociology of Power in Africa*. London: James Currey. Portsmouth: Heinemann Educational Books.

Cohen, D.W. & E.S. Atieno-Odhiambo. (1989). *Siaya: The Historical Anthropology of an African Landscape*. Athens: Ohio University Press.

Ehret, C. (2001). 'The Eastern Kenya Interior', in Atieno-Odhiambo, E. S. (ed.) *African Historians and African Voices: Essays Presented to Professor Bethwell Allan Ogot on His Seventieth Birthday*. Switzerland: P. Schlettwein Publishing.

Giday, B. (1992). *Ethiopian Civilization*. Addis Ababa. http://africanhi story.about.com/od/Kenya/p/KenyaHist.htm. Accessed on [08 September, 2011].

Iliffe, J. (1987). *The African Poor*. Cambridge: Cambridge University Press.

Iliffe, J. (1995). *Africans: The History of a Continent*. Cambridge: Cambridge University Press.

Low, D. A. (1971). *The Mind of Buganda: Documents of the Modern History of an African Kingdom*. London, Ibadan and Nairobi: Heinemann.

Mngomezulu, B. R. (2004). 'A Political History of Higher Education in East Africa, 1937-1970.' Unpublished PhD thesis, Rice University.

Mngomezulu, B. R. (2006). 'An Assessment of the Role Played by Political Leaders, Nationalism and Sub-Nationalisms in the Establishment and Collapse of the East African Community, 1960-1977'. Masters Dissertation, University of South Africa.

Mngomezulu, B. R. (2008). 'Leadership Crisis in Africa: Contextualising African Leaders' Obsession With Power,' in *Journal of Business and Management Dynamics* Vol.2, December.

Njoh, A. J. (2006). *Tradition, Culture and Development in Africa.* Burlington: Ashgate.

Ochieng', D. W. (1987). *An Outline History of Nyanza Up to 1914.* Nairobi: Kenya literature Bureau.

_____(1986). *People of the South-Western highlands: Gusii.* Nairobi: Evans Brothers, United Kingdom: Hodder Headline.

_____. (1979). *People around the Lake (Kenya's People).* United Kingdom: Evans Brothers.

_____. (1975). *A History of the Kadimo Chiefdom of the Yimbo in Western Kenya.* Nairobi: East African Literature Bureau.

_____. (1974). *An Outline History Of The Rift Valley Of Kenya.* Nairobi: East African Bureau.

Odhiambo, E. S. (2001). (ed.). *African Historians and African Voices: Essays Presented to Professor Bethwell Allan Ogot on His Seventieth Birthday.* Switzerland: P.Schlettwein Publishing.

Ogot, B. A. (2009). *History of the Luo-Speaking Peoples of Eastern Africa.* Nairobi: East African Publishing House.

_____. (2002)._The Challenges of History and Leadership in Africa: The Essays of Bethwell Allan Ogot.* Africa World Press.

_____. (1999a). *Africa from the Sixteenth to the Eighteenth Century.* UNESCO.

_____. (1999b). *Reintroducing Man into the African World: Selected Essays 1961-80.* Kisumu: Anyange Press.

_____. (1982). 'The Silences in the Old Narratives, Or, New Trends in Cultural History. *Journal of eastern African Research & Development.* 12: 36-45.

_____.(1976). *Kenya before 1900.* Nairobi: East African publishing House.

_____.J.A. Kieran (eds.) (1968). *Zamani: A Survey of East African History.* Nairobi: East African Publishing House.

_____. (1967). *History of the Southern Luo: Volume I, Migration and Settlement, 1500-1900.* Nairobi: East African Publishing House.

Rake, A. (2001). *African Leaders: Guiding the New Millennium.* London: The Scarecrow Press.

Russell, A. (1999). *Big Men, Little People: The Leaders Who Defined Africa.* New York: New York University Press.

Van Rensburg, A. P. (1981). *Africa's Men of Destiny.* Bloemfontein: De Jager-Haum.

CHAPTER 3: ZIMBABWE

Mugabe: Reinvention and Political Survival in Zimbabwe

Marshall Tamuka Maposa

THE MAP OF ZIMBABWE

3.1 Introduction

The advent of independence in 1980 ushered in a new political era for the people of Zimbabwe. A middle-aged Robert Mugabe had managed to manoeuvre the skirmishes and backbiting that constituted the struggle for independence and emerged as Prime Minister and leader of the new country. Coming into power as a former guerrilla leader, he surprised many of his detractors with his conciliatory approach at independence. Such was his ability to transform his image that he at the outset represented a new hope for an independent African country (a hope which had recurrently been dashed elsewhere on the African continent). However, the personality that charmed the world then has since turned out to be a subject of contention as almost 33 years later he still remains in power, but now representing a rather different face from the earlier one. This chapter analyses Mugabe's ability since becoming the country's executive president in 1987 to reinvent himself in a manner that has capacitated him to still be in power when men and women who were born in his first term of office are now fully mature adults and others have already passed away over the years.

It should be noted right from the outset that Mugabe's political longevity cannot be credited to him alone as some would want us to believe. Such insinuation would be both misleading and parochial in all respects. Rather, many varied factors (and indeed the absence of some in other instances) have individually and jointly contributed to his political survival which has stood firm for more than three decades even when Britain and America relentlessly called for his resignation each time his term of office came to an end. Noticeably, not even economic sanctions have been successful in moving Mugabe; he has stood firm and became even much stronger than ever before. However, the scope of this chapter will focus on Mugabe's reinvention, simply because the other factors are too vast to be analysed fairly within the limitations of this chapter. I firstly review a selection of some of the literature that helped to motivate and create a framework for my analysis and then move on to discuss Mugabe as a guerrilla before he assumed the position of power as Prime Minister and, later, as executive president of the country. Subsequently, I discuss how Mugabe used that power to sustain himself and prolong his stay in office despite opposition.

3.2 Literature Review and Theory

In an attempt to tackle the subject of this chapter, I first consulted various forms of literature, but mainly books, journal articles and newspaper archives to make sense of the phenomenon of political survival and apply it to Zimbabwe's Robert Mugabe. While a significant amount has been written on Mugabe in particular and Zimbabwe in general from different perspectives the general trend is to describe his dictatorial characteristics in a rather mundane fashion, particularly in the first decade of the 21st century. In this chapter, political survival is used interchangeably with political longevity. It is de Clercy (2007), who views political longevity to be synonymous with political survival and who defines it as "a politician's ability to retain his or her position as party leader." This view is rather different from the one held by Bueno de Mesquita, Siverson, Smith, and Morrow (2007: 436) who summarily contend that "all leaders survive." Their argument is that politics is a matter of survival and whether one lasts in power for a week or forty years, they will have put effort to retain power since challengers are always there to take their chances in a bid to ascend to the highest position and take charge by all means possible. The concept of political survival is not very widely researched in both social and political sciences and therefore this gap substantiates the rationale for this chapter. However, this gap does not necessarily imply that political survival is a novel phenomenon. Indeed, Machiavelli's *The Prince* discusses this concept amongst others in an eloquent manner.

As they emerged from colonialism, a number of African countries ended up under the control of one-party and unlimited-tenure governments. It was only in the early 1990s that one-party liberation governments began to crumble and make way for democratically elected leaders. This was the case, for example, in Kenya with the 1992 Constitutional amendment and in Nigeria with the 1999 Constitution. That wave of democracy also resulted in diminishing terms of incumbents - something that was not considered earlier. But it is important to note that such a development is not limited to Africa alone. In fact the worldwide trend is that there is evident decline in the time leaders spend at the helm of both political parties and countries (de Clercy, 2007). In spite of this trend, a few leaders still manage to prolong their time at the helm somehow.

Various factors enable politicians to hold on to power. Invariably, the factors are dependent on the specific contextual realities. With a focus on Canada, de Clercy (2007) identifies as factors determining the political longevity of leaders, issues such as intraparty tension and poor performance in elections. This view places the factors in the hands of the leader and his party and how they perform. It should be argued that there are factors not necessarily directly linked to the ruling party that also contribute to the political survival of the incumbent. In another conceptual study, Bueno de Mesquita et al (2007), identify three variables: the country's economic fortunes, leaders and their challengers' political competence, the levels of affinities between the electoral candidate and the electorate. This acknowledges variables from across the political spectrum as contributing to political longevity. The existence of a multiplicity of factors is not accepted by all scholars. For example, in the view of Anthony Downs whatever action political leaders take, the real reason behind it is to help them remain in power. For Kenneth (2009), an analysis of African politicians usually leads to at least two conclusions: that the leaders are able to adapt to changing contextual factors, or that the democratic systems in the specific countries are inherently weak and allow manipulation by the incumbents. Certainly, it is safe to say that the reasons for this manipulation vary from one leader to the next as much as they differ from country to country at any given time.

The theme of this book is on life presidents in Africa who do not want to relinquish power even when all signs show that they have run their race and have to step aside and allow fellow countrymen and women to take the country forward. But how long does one have to hang on to power to be considered a 'life president'? A sample given by Bueno de Mesquita et al (2007) is used as a guideline in this chapter. They described as cases of political survivors, "individuals who were among the twenty-five longest lasting leaders since 1955 in countries with a population of at least one million without regard for whether they performed well in producing peace, prosperity, and civil and political freedom for the average citizen" Bueno de Mesquita (2007: 433). The sample produced an average tenure of 35.1 years. Using this sample as a guideline I argue that, while 'life president' might be a debatable designation for someone who did not die (or has not yet died) in office, in this case it refers to a leader who rules for over a generation. That means that when a leader clocks 25 consecutive years in power they have demonstrated high levels of political longevity. In the case of Mugabe, it is now over 30 years; in a country where life expectancy statistics were revealed by the United Nations to have descended to below forty, the Zimbabwean leader can be claimed to have been in charge for a lifetime.

Setting the scene for an analysis of Mugabe's political survival, Kenneth (2009) uses the metaphor of the baobab tree to describe the President of Cameroon, Paul Biya's political longevity as he negotiated his way through pressures from within and without. What is seen to be the key to Biya's political survival is his "overnight conversion" to democracy when he realised that he could not hold on to power through repression (Kenneth, 2009: 3). The overnight conversion referred to here might be more apparent than real, but it works in favour of the politician as it presents a reinvented individual, albeit with the old characteristics now hidden. While Biya might be argued to have reinvented himself once as he negotiated the democratic quests of the 1990s it will be shown here albeit very briefly that his contemporary, Mugabe, has actually reinvented his character more than once during his political career. Nevertheless, running across these reinventions is a common thread which is epitomised by the ultimate goal of prolonging his political tenure. Tracing Mugabe's political activities will shed some light as to why he thinks it is right for him to cling on to power for this long. In this regard, his different faces will be revealed in order to bring to the fore different nodal points which describe Mugabe and which must be fully understood if one is to do justice in analysing him as a political figure. As stated earlier in this chapter, previous authors have focused on one side of Mugabe and to a large degree paid more attention to the period when Mugabe had already started portraying himself as a monster and not the likeable leader he used to be when he ascended to power. Some of these points are expounded below and they date back to the time of the liberation struggle which predates the 1980 liberation which is commonly used as the starting point in most writings on Mugabe and Zimbabwe.

3.3 Mugabe the Guerrilla

The designation of Mugabe as a guerrilla is a term of contention, mainly as there is no real evidence of him being involved in any combat. However as soon as he cemented his position as leader of the Zimbabwe African National Union (ZANU) in 1977, he effectively took charge of the guerrilla movement which had been spearheaded by ZANU's military wing, the Zimbabwe African Nationalist Army (ZANLA). By assuming leadership of ZANU, Mugabe by default became commander of ZANLA and ex-officio leader of Dare reChimurenga (Revolutionary Command Council) (Tekere, 2007).

It is with such weighty portfolios that Mugabe assumed the leadership of the country at independence. By taking over from Ndabaningi Sithole (who was viewed to be moderate) Mugabe seemed to be the hardliner that the purveyors of the war had waited for, while for those on the opposite side he seemed to be another communist guerrilla taking over the country and overturning the entire system of government (Baxter, 2010). Such fears were so real that at the announcement of the independence election results, a stream of predominantly white citizens found its way out of the country anticipating political instability and possible persecution of the white people. The chief destination of these emigrating whites was South Africa (Meredith, 2009).

It is clear from this synopsis that Mugabe became the prominent leader by default. If that is indeed true then it means that he knew that there would be many people who would challenge his position of authority. To prevent this from happening he had to choose between being harsh against prospective claimants to the leadership position or pretend to be accommodating them in his leadership circle. As alluded to above, Mugabe tried both methods interchangeably as time and space allowed. Some would blame him for his dual approach to the potential crisis but the primary goal was political survival. For these almost dubious actions there are those who started to portray Mugabe as a statesman in the real sense of the word. Whether this was indeed a fair and objective assessment of this leader, remains a debatable subject. But a question could be phrased as follows: What did the portrayal of Mugabe as a statesman entail? This question is addressed below.

3.4 Mugabe the Statesman

It should be noted that the roots of Mugabe's political survival had been sown as he took over the reins of ZANU through a not so clean process (a discussion which does not fall under the focus of this chapter). However, the man's first reinvention was at hand at independence. Mugabe's party won the elections and he was sworn into power as Prime Minister of Zimbabwe, while the President, Canaan Banana, was appointed symbolically in a virtually ceremonial role. At his maiden speech as Prime Minister, Mugabe both shocked and impressed supporters and detractors alike with his 'swords to ploughshares' speech. The reconciliatory tone of the speech announced to the world a reinvented Mugabe - the statesman of high calibre. Evidently he seemed to have learned from the experiences of other post-colonial African countries such as Mozambique. Indeed, it is argued that, amongst others, Mozambican President Samora Machel and Julius Nyerere of Tanzania had advised Mugabe against retribution to avoid chaos in the newly independent country (Mandaza, (1986). By heeding the advice of these leaders Mugabe confirmed that indeed he was a statesman and not just a greedy and heartless political leader as others assumed him to be.

It is worth mentioning that the image of Mugabe as a statesman was not limited to speeches alone. In practice, he surprisingly impressed those who had thought the worst of him. Even his erstwhile enemy and former Rhodesian Prime Minister, Ian Smith, could not believe what he saw and remarked that: "He behaved like a balanced, civilised Westerner, the antithesis of the communist gangster I had expected" (Meredith, 2007: 42). Such observations and confessions may, on one hand, be interpreted to be evidence of misconceptions that Rhodesians had of liberation fighters. On the other hand, they may be viewed as evidence of 'overnight conversion' from Mugabe the guerrilla to Mugabe the statesman. Whichever is the case, such a reinvention played a role in Mugabe's political survival as he got both domestic and international support on his side. Domestic support was crucially significant as even some of the white farmers who had packed their bags and got ready to migrate to countries like South Africa to join others decided to stay as there was hope for a positive future and no sign of Zimbabwe being a bloodbath as they had anticipated.

Other examples of Mugabe's evident reinvention at independence are manifested by the system of government that he followed in 1980 at independence. Undeniably, he had to compromise since the independence conditions had to be settled at the negotiation table in Lancaster House in the United Kingdom. Still, the new government was inclusive of the diverse political parties and demographic groups of the country. In addition, the constitution guaranteed the separation of the arms of government and the supremacy of parliament over the executive. It has been argued around many circles that the inclusivity which Mugabe implemented in 1980 was a template that Nelson Mandela used 14 years later when he came to power in South Africa following the demise of apartheid. If Mandela is celebrated as a statesman up to today, then it can also be contented that Mugabe was a statesman in 1980 when he claimed the leadership of the country. Statesmanship enhances one's chances of political survival since it brings all the politically important role-players to one's side instead of turning them against him. This was the case during the early days of Daniel arap Moi's presidency in Kenya as discussed by Mngomezulu in the previous chapter of this manuscript.

Mugabe's rein as Prime Minister lasted until 1987. Up to that time, he can still be described as a statesman as was manifested by his support at home and abroad. At home he swept through the 1985 elections as his party won 77% of the votes, which was a great improvement from the 63% his party obtained in the 1980 election (Sithole, 1997). Internationally, Mugabe received awards including honorary degrees from the Universities of Edinburgh and Massachusetts. It could be argued then that Mugabe's position as leader of Zimbabwe was secure both at home and abroad. But as discussed in Chapter 1 of this book, Edinburgh University later took the degree back when it discovered that Mugabe once orchastrated the killing of about 20, 000 people in Joshua Nkomo's home province, Matabeleland.

However, behind this veil of statesmanship is evidence of what Kenneth (2007:4), referred to as "feigned conversion." Traits of Mugabe the guerrilla still permeated through the period no matter how hard he tried to suppress them. In fact Meredith (2009) claims that the honeymoon period after independence lasted for at least three years. Just as he had managed to rise to the top of the liberation struggle structures, Mugabe had to use his survival skills to eliminate potential threats to his position. The period from about 1983 to 1987 witnessed a government sponsored military onslaught in the Midlands and Matabeleland regions ostensibly because dissidents had to be stopped from terrorising the villagers and farmers (Sibanda, 2005). Up to the present-day, there has not been any official investigation into this campaign which was code-named *Gukurahundi*. The government's version of the causes, course and effects of *Gukurahundi* has been notably mute save for Mugabe's admission that it was "a moment of madness" (Daimon, 2002:1). Although the *Gukurahundi* saga was quickly swept under the carpet for political reasons, it is a manifestation of Mugabe's feigned conversion into a statesman which helped him retain his position for much longer.

In addition to the *Gukurahundi* issue, the government had remained fundamentally socialist. It might not have been as leftist as had been promised the ordinary population during the war of liberation, but the reconciliatory sentiments illustrated earlier could not veil the fundamentally socialist nature of government. Mugabe's implementation of socialism has been discussed and in some cases dismissed, but Law (2009: 49), argues that the period 1980 to 1985 was characterised by "episodes of ambiguity" whereby the government seemed to genuinely believe in a socialist future for the country. It can be argued that the socialist tinge was a necessary tool to keep the disadvantaged hopeful about the future. The bottom-line is that Mugabe was able to use it as a weapon to secure political survival by getting interest groups on his side both locally and internationally. These two perceptions of Mugabe and the way in which he successfully played both roles at different political moments mean that he was an adaptable figure - a point discussed in the next sub-heading.

3.5 Mugabe the Adaptable Character

The end of *Gukurahundi* heralded a new political era in Zimbabwean politics. The frustrations of the 1980s had in some cases shown how an irritable Mugabe, can be intolerant to opposition. However, his statesman-like character discussed above papered over the cracks and secured him political longevity. By 1987, he changed into a more adaptable character as a result of the local and international realities influencing the Zimbabwean political landscape. Consequently he was able to comfortably survive what is usually referred to as the 'third wave of democratisation', which resulted in many of Africa's longstanding leaders and dictators losing power during the 1990s (Kenneth, 2007: 1). Mugabe had managed to build up on his earlier position such that the population became largely apathetic either due to contentment, disillusionment or ambivalence. According to the ZESN (2008), the evidence of voter apathy is that "from an estimated turnout of 94 % in 1980, the proportion declined steadily over the years to 84% in 1985 and 47% in 1990." It was this apathy that also enabled Mugabe to reinvent himself as a fluid character as shall be described shortly. It should also not be forgotten that Mugabe has lately adopted a strategy of persecuting the electorate in those areas supporting opposition leaders to ensure that they do not vote. He perfected this plan by sending the police and the army to carry out this dirty work for him and rewarded them for doing that both materially and financially.

The end of *Gukurahundi* was followed by the signing of the Unity Accord of 1987 which saw ZANU unite with ZAPU (Zimbabwe African Peoples' Union) led by veteran nationalist and Mugabe's now major rival Joshua Nkomo to form ZANU PF. Zimbabwe was virtually a one-party state and for a while Mugabe pushed this agenda because the strategy worked for him. It was disturbed by the existence of one parliamentary seat occupied by Mugabe's ZANU predecessor, Ndabaningi Sithole, who by now had been openly side-lined from the mainstream Zimbabwean political and historical narrative (Sithole, 1997). Any further hopes of one-party state were dashed when by the 1990 election a new political party, the Zimbabwe Unity Movement (ZUM) had been formed by Mugabe's former comrade, Edgar Tekere, who had pulled out of ZANU.

Nevertheless the failure of the one-party state did not threaten Mugabe's political survival then. In any case, he had taken advantage of the increasing apathy to consolidate his position by executing what were arguably the first major constitutional amendments after independence. The amendments of 1987 abolished the position of Prime Minister and created the Executive Presidency which Mugabe would take over (Sachikonye, 2001). This rebranding was rationalised by the argument that executive powers would enable the new President to make quick decisions and hence cut bureaucracy and increase efficiency. The new title alone gave a fresh outlook and new hopes and was instrumental in promoting Mugabe's political longevity as he would be judged from the new title that he had assumed not the previous ones which left his name tainted. Other power-consolidating constitutional changes in this period included the abolition of the separate voters' roll for whites; the abolition of the Senate resulting in the existence of only one parliamentary body; and the appointment of the Attorney General as a cabinet member, thus ensuring executive influence over the judiciary (Sachikonye, 2001). These amendments, just like many others to be conducted later, did not undergo any sort of referendum for public approval. In the process of reinventing himself as Executive President, Mugabe had ensured his political survival without any doubt.

In this period, the world was changing. The Soviet Union dissolved, the Berlin Wall fell and the communist world was in a fluster. Zimbabwe had to reposition herself and contextualise into these changes as well. At the same time, the third wave of democracy was sweeping across Africa. Locally, signs of corruption had reared an ugly head with the Willowgate scandal of 1989 leading to the resignation of cabinet ministers and even the death of one. The government had also invested heavily in social services such as health and education. This investment, coupled with increasing corruption, created an economic situation whereby Zimbabwe began to struggle paying off her debts something which was not common before.

With these new challenges Mugabe had to stay ahead of the game otherwise it was gradually becoming clear that his days in office were numbered. Subsequently, more constitutional changes followed. The next big amendment was in 1990 when the term of the President was revised upwards to six years (Zimbabwe Constitution, 2008). This meant that the next parliamentary elections would be held in 1995 with the presidential poll taking place the following year. This was a proactive political survival strategy. The parliamentary election would be a good gauge of the political orientation and attitudes of the electorate so that he could prepare well for the presidential election. This was not really necessary in 1995 and 1996 as apathy increased, but this set-up would be useful in the next election as shall be discussed later in this chapter.

If Mugabe had adopted a straightjacket approach in the late 1980s and early 1990s he would have sacrificed his position sooner or later. The socialist slant was slowly disposed of as he gave in to the temptation of capitalist aid and loans. This was in response to the reality his country was facing at the time. The appeal for loans from the International Monetary Fund (IMF) and the World Bank (WB) was a manifestation of an ideology shift. As a result, Mugabe who had come to power as a socialist guerrilla leader had turned to capitalism by adopting the Economic Structural Adjustment Programme (ESAP) in 1991 (Carmody & Taylor, 2003). This was another conversion that Mugabe had gone through, coming in with new ideological promises for the people of Zimbabwe. This adaptation can also be argued to be a feigned conversion as ESAP was abandoned as a failure in 1995. From 1987 to 1997 the adaptations were coming faster, all with the ultimate result of consolidating Mugabe's political longevity.

By 1997 the apathy of the populace was evidently turning out to be more out of disappointment rather than contentment or ambivalence (Sithole, 1997). But before then Mugabe's position was secure. Indeed, he kept winning further awards, such as the Africa Prize for Leadership for the Sustainable End of Hunger in 1988 (French, 1988) and the Knight Grand Cross in the Order of the Bath in 1994 (Lawson, 2007). This international support was crucial in Mugabe's political survival at home. The latter award was more so as he had reinvented himself towards the Britain-inclined ideology of capitalism. In a way, this was Britain's positive gesture in appreciation of Mugabe's repentance.

3.6 Mugabe the Post-Colonial African Pugilist

Probably, the greatest reinvention Mugabe had to do was in the late 1990s. More than 15 years after taking over power, the strain of past mistakes and prolonged tenure began to show. The ambivalence and disappointment of the populace increasingly turned into outright disillusionment. As a result, strikes and riots became more regular. The biggest corruption scandal after Willowgate was the War Veterans Compensation Fund outrage. Evidence came out from various sources that most of the ZANU PF members of government had received absurd amounts as compensation for the injuries and losses they incurred during the liberation struggle while the ordinary veterans who had stayed out of politics were subjects of ridicule because of their impoverished position (Kriger, 2005). The Zimbabwe National Liberation War Veterans Association (ZNLWVA) led by Chenjerai Hunzvi suddenly became a nuisance to Mugabe as they demanded their share of compensation. Mugabe's government realised that the war veterans were not just a nuisance but a potential source of opposition and so they were compensated with gratuities of ZW$50 000 each and promised a monthly pension allowance. This was Mugabe's attempt to silence them so that he could focus on other potential contenders to his position.

The solution to the war veterans' demands turned out to have started a domino. The same war veterans joined poor villagers in demanding for land which they claimed had been the leading motivation behind the liberation war. Inflation was increasing as a result of the increased balance of payments with the International Monetary Fund (IMF) and the World Bank. At the same time, the unbudgeted, but politically expedient war compensation disbursements contributed significantly to the rise of inflation. By 1998, the major cities were rocked with riots over food shortages. Meanwhile, the new Labour government in Britain refused to take responsibility for the compensation for land reform as they claimed they had nothing to do with Conservative agreements (Zimbabwe Government, 2003). Many other problems beset the country at the end of the century, but discussing all of them here would be moving away from the focus of the chapter. They will therefore be left out.

With the increasing problems, Mugabe had to be more reactive than remaining proactive as he had been earlier in his reign. The early farm invaders from the Svosve villages led by Chief Enock Zenda Gahadza (Svosve) were threatened by the promise that they would be moved from the farms by the army and the police. However, the government soon realised how important land was to the rural population and how the rural farm invaders were gaining support from the war veterans (Wels, 2003) and some urban dwellers that were moving quickly towards the formation of an opposition political party. By all accounts, this new development posed an imminent threat to Mugabe's position. By 1999, the Movement for Democratic Change (MDC) had been launched with most of its support from traditional anti-Mugabe constituencies, the youth, the urban dwellers and the white farmers. Civic organisations such as the National Constitutional Assembly (NCA) also added their voice for either reform or the outright ouster of Mugabe (Sachikonye, 2007). To deal with these threatening issues, Mugabe reinvented himself as post-colonial African pugilist.

In his new conversion, Mugabe had to follow the interests of the land demanders and the war veterans. This entails leaving out the urban population. But simple statistics showed that there were more people in the rural areas than in towns and cities. Mugabe chose to run with the apparent majority and sell them the idea of land. Suddenly, he amplified his rhetoric towards white Zimbabwean farmers and virtually all Western governments, particularly, the American and British leaders. This rhetoric was epitomised by Mugabe's rallying cry: "Zimbabwe will never be a colony again." The implication was that Western powers had neo-colonial interests in Zimbabwe and he was the defender of the people of Zimbabwe. The attacks on Mugabe and his government, including his sanctioning by Western powers only gave him more fuel for his African pugilist course which he had converted to. Those who bought his arguments now saw Mugabe as a victim of Western demonization and conspiracies rather than seeing him as responsible for the issues the country was facing. The more Zimbabwe sunk into crisis, the more anti-Western imperialism the government produced and disseminated via the state-controlled media. Mugabe rode on this ticket right up to the 2008 'harmonised election' which ended up being declared by the AU and other bodies as a farce. In fact, he used his apparent role as defence for the problems that characterised the 2008 election. As a result, in spite of losing the election, and running in a one-man run-off election, he still got some support in some sections of the AU and the Southern African Development Community (SADC). This was very sad because, in a way, those AU and SADC members who supported Mugabe approved his treacherous activities. By all accounts, if Mugabe was a culprit in stealing the elections, it goes without saying that those who endorsed him as having been dully elected were accomplices in that crime. Such indictment is inevitable from an analytic point of view.

3.7 Conclusion: The Final Reinvention?

Many political analysts predicted the ouster of Mugabe since 2000. Noticeably, he still remains at the helm as president of Zimbabwe with the man who beat him in the contentious first round settling for a weaker Prime Minister post in the Government of National Unity (GNU) which was set up by the Global Political Agreement (GPA) of 2008. How this happened is a question many find hard to comprehend.

The country at present has a GNU like it had at independence. Mugabe has not gone back to his conciliatory stance of 1980 though. He still plays the post-colonial African pugilist role, which however, is watered down as he now has to rely on international recognition for legitimacy. There were speculations that only time would tell if he could reinvent himself again with the elections set for 2012. It is now 2013 and Mugabe is still holding the reigns with few signs (if any at all) that he will vacate office. This point is compounded by the fact that the turn of events since the 1990s left Mugabe even more vicious. The emergence of political parties such as the MDC and evident attempts to challenge Mugabe openly for the leadership position have forced him to use all the resources at his disposal to cling on to power.

What cannot be denied is the fact that no matter how one perceives him, Robert Mugabe is a political survivor. The countries in the SADC region have had at least 3 different leaders in the time that he alone has been at the helm in Zimbabwe. This is an enviable achievement of sort. In this chapter, I analysed Mugabe's political longevity based on the theories of political survival. I argued that Mugabe's tenure as leader of Zimbabwe has been prolonged, amongst other things, because he has been able to consistently reinvent and rebrand himself pending the situation he finds himself in. As such, I divided his reign into about five reinventions. It emerged that in his early days, his reinvention was proactive, but as he began to face complex challenges he started to be adaptable until he became fully reactive. I acknowledge that there are many other factors that contribute to his prolonged tenure, but they all cannot be discussed within the scope of this chapter. The aim of the chapter was simply to demonstrate how Mugabe has succeeded in retaining his position as President of Zimbabwe for more than three decades. The discussion above has attempted to answer this question, albeit inconclusively due to time and space. However, the answers provided here are useful in resolving the impulse surrounding Mugabe and his continued stay in political office for such a long time.

References

Baxter, P. (2010). *Rhodesia: Last Outpost of the British Empire Alberton*: Galago Publishing Pty Ltd.

Bueno de Mesquita, B., Smith, A., Siverson, R.M. & Morrow, J. D. (2002). *The Logic of Political Survival* (Publisher unknown).

Carmody, & Taylor. Industry and the urban sector in Zimbabwe's political economy. African studies quarterly,(7)2&3. Retrieved, 15 July 2011, from http://web.africa.ufl.edu/asq/v7/v7i2a3.htm.

Constitution of Zimbabwe (2007).

Daimon, A. (2002). "The Matabeleland massacres/Gukurahundi were a moment of madness": Forgetful memory and contestations over historical truth and justice in Zimbabwe's 1st post-colonial genocide.

De Clercy, C. Declining political survival rates among parliamentary party leaders, 1867-2006: A federal and provincial trend. Paper presented to the annual meetings of the Canadian Political Science Association. University of Saskatchewan, Saskatoon, Saskatchewan, May 20, 2007.

Kriger, N. (2005). "Veterans' pensions in Zimbabwe: dispute resolution and nation-building". *Ohio State Journal on Dispute Resolution*.

Law, K. (2009). Episodes of ambiguity: Steps towards socialism in Zimbabwe, 1980-1985. *ARAS*, 30(1).

Mandaza, I. (1987). *The Political Economy of Transition, 1980-1986.* Harare: Zimbabwe Publishing House.

Meredith, M. (2009). *Mugabe: Power, Plunder and the Struggle for Zimbabwe*. Johannesburg: Jonathan Ball.

Ngwa Anye Kenneth, N.G. (2009). The baobab tree lives on: Paul Biya and the logic of political survival. Johns Hopkins SAIS: African Studies Department.

Sachikonye, L. (2011). Zimbabwe's constitution-making and electoral reform processes: challenges and opportunities. Draft paper prepared for the Conference on 'Legitimacy of Power-Possibilities of Opposition' Organised by Department of Political Science and Public Administration, Makerere University and Chr. Michelson Institute (CMI), May 30- June 1, 2011.

Tekere, E.Z. (2007). *A Lifetime of Struggle*. Sappes.

Walker, S. G. (2004). Review: Leaders and the logic of political survival. International Studies Review, 6(3) 486-488.Retrieved 15 July 2011, from http://www.jstor.org/stable/3699711.

Sithole, M. & Makumbe, J. (1997). "Elections in Zimbabwe: The ZANU (PF) hegemony and its incipient decline". *African Journal of Political Science*, 2(1), 122-139

Wels, H. (2008). *Private Wildlife Conservation in Zimbabwe: Joint Ventures and Reciprocity*. [Publisher unknown).

Zimbabwe election support network [ZESN]. (2008). Report on the Zimbabwe 29 march harmonized election and 27 June 2008 presidential run-off.

CHAPTER 4: NIGERIA

The Perpetuation of the Long Stay in Office by Nigerian Political Leaders

Louis Okon Akpan

THE MAP OF NIGERIA

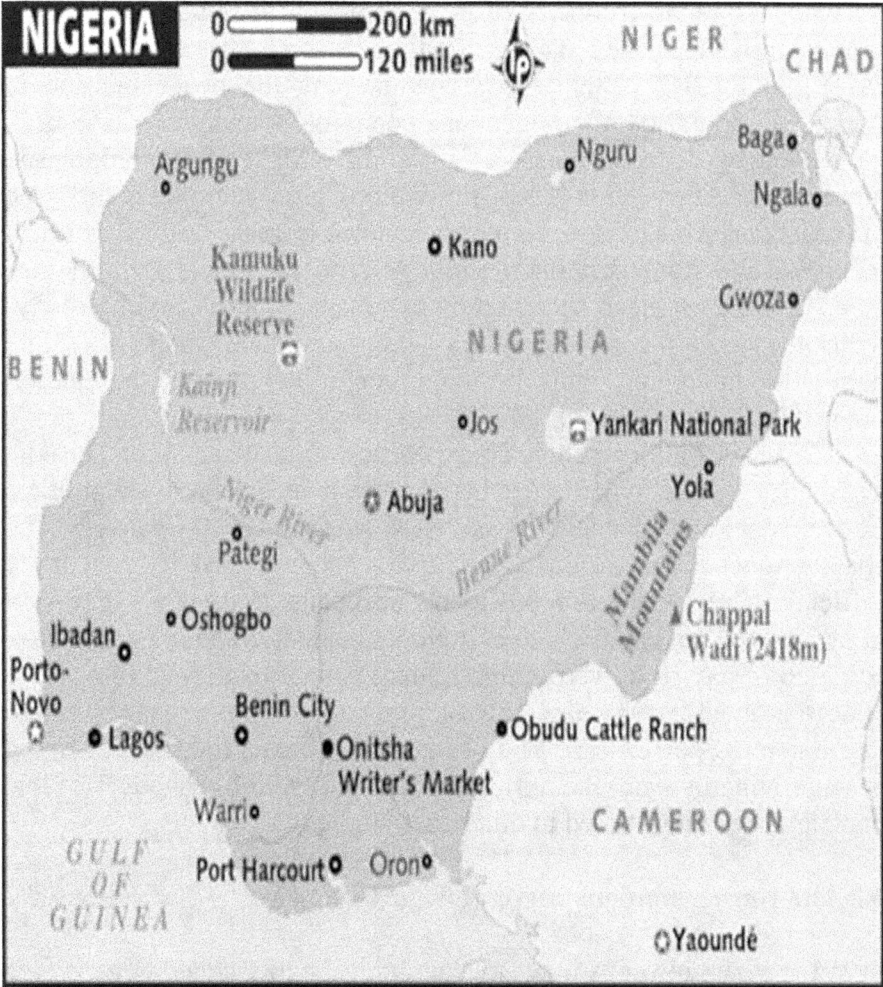

4.1 Introduction

Nigeria, by virtue of her large population, which was approximately 167 million in 2012, is regarded as the giant of Africa. On the international scene, Nigeria has contributed immensely to the stabilisation of most of the African countries over the past few decades (Akinterinwa, 2005; Udogu, 2005; Garba, 1987). For instance, Nigeria played a prominent role by ensuring that peace returned to Liberia, Sierra Leone, Ivory Coast, and Democratic Republic of Congo (DRC). Recently, Nigerian troops have been deployed in Sudan for a peace keeping mission. They have served under both the African Union (AU) and the UN. But despite championing the peace mission in Africa, Nigeria's social, political and economic foundations have been threatened by different forms of instability. Most of these domestic problems faced are, in fact, self-inflicted. A clear example is the issue of leadership which has been a mirage since Nigeria attained political independence from Britain in 1960. Nigeria's political terrain since independence has been occupied by callous, visionless, and narrowly-focussed people whose main aim of being in office was to embezzle public funds to suit their personal needs and render the masses impoverished.

The basis for this scholarly expedition is to discuss the periodic destruction of the Nigerian political terrain by a clique of political leaders since independence who were obsessed with power. The chapter touches on various uncivilised channels used by Aso Rock (official office of Nigerian president) occupants to elongate their stay in office even beyond their constitutional mandate. The impact of their continuous stay in power is highlighted to help readers have a better understanding of why this is bad practice for the country. In the discussion, Nigerian case is linked to the broader African context because Nigeria is not the only culprit as discussed in chapter 1 of this book and as demonstrated in other case studies.

4.2 The Unceremonious Birth of Nigeria

In 1914, what now constitutes a geographical entity called Nigeria was born. Sir Lord Fredrick Lugard amalgamated what used to be the Southern and Northern Protectorates into one country which was subsequently named Nigeria. This 'forced marriage' between the two protectorates was neither defined nor mutually agreed upon by the natives of the area at the time. There is documentary evidence which shows that this 'unholy marriage' was contracted by the colonial masters in order to exploit and appropriate the enormous wealth found in Nigeria. This should be understood in the context of British hegemony and practices as epitomized by the Central African Federation and the East African Community referred to in various chapters in this book.

In 1939, for reason best known to colonialists, the southern part of the region was further divided into two: the East and West and in 1956 Nigeria, still under colonial rule, was federated with very strong units of the North, East and West. The North covered about four quarters of the country's total landmass and equally accounted for about half the total population of the country. To-date, Nigeria has about 250 distinct ethnic groups and the dominant ones are Hausa, Igbo, Yoruba, Ibibio and Ijaws. Whilst the Igbo, Yoruba, Ibibio and Ijaws reside in the Sothern part of the country, the Northern section of Nigeria is occupied by the Hausa.

After strong and persistent agitation and struggle for independence by some distinguished and notable leaders, such as Dr. Nnamdi Azikiwe, Sir Tafewa Balewa, Sir Ahmadu Bello, Chief Awolowo and Chief Udoma Udo Udoma, the British Union Jack (Flag) was lowered and in its place the Nigerian National Flag was hoisted signalling the birth of Nigeria on October 1, 1960. Under a conservative federal coalition government which was formed and led by Dr. Azikiwe as Governor General, the new nation state began the decolonisation process of the entire country. This democratic process was short-lived because the coalition government formed was not able to live above ethnic and tribal enclaves. Madunagu (2001) argues that within two years of independence the political agreements which produced the Federal Government had broken down and what looked like an experiment in democracy had been extinguished. But the regime dragged on for three more years before its final demise.

4.3 Nigeria's Power Game Of 1966

In the morning of Saturday, January 15, 1966, a 28 year old major in the Nigerian Army in the person of Chukwuma Kundan Nzeogwu violently staged a coup d'état. As was generally the norm in most

African countries, the independence Constitution was suspended and in its place the Supreme Council of the Revolution was instituted. The main reason given for the overthrow of the first civilian administration by those young army boys was that it was tainted by corruption. Part of the excerpts of Nzeogwu's broadcast read thus:

> Our enemies are the political profiteers, the swindlers, the men in high and low places that seek bribes and demand ten per cent, those that seek to keep the country divided permanently so that they can remain in office as ministers of VIPs at least, the tribalists, the nepotists, those that make the country look for big nothing before international circles, those that corrupted our society and put the Nigerian political calendar back by their words and deeds.

This organ of the then government acted as the Legislative House whose main objectives, as Bassey (1996) submits, was to establish a country which was strong, united and prosperous, free from corruption and internal strife. This marked the genesis of military intervention in the Nigerian political terrain.

The Nzeogwu-led coup was a complete success in the Northern part of Nigerian, particularly Kaduna where some top government officials were killed. But the coup was a complete failure in the South, specifically in Lagos because the top government officials targeted for elimination escaped. Since the coup was partially successful, there was apprehension by the Northerners that the coup was organised to silence their leaders. With the collapse of these popular uprisings, the coup leader was finally surrendered to General Ironsi who was the most senior officer in the Nigerian army. Nzeogwu was subsequently arrested and taken to Lagos for questioning. With him were other culprits who had assisted him in staging the coup.

Before his arrest and his journey to Lagos, Nzeogwu reached an agreement with Ironsi, through his military boys that those top government officials who were removed from office should not be returned to power and that he and his compatriots should be accorded a "safe conduct". It is worthy of note that this agreement between Nzeogwu and General Ironsi was never kept. Nzeogwu and his boys were kept in detention. Ironsi's victory was not just a defeat for a revolution and a return to the old status quo. Madunagu (2001), held that his victory became a powerful weapon in the hands of those who sought to discredit the Nzeogwu-led revolution. The domination of the conspiratorial group by officers of the Igbo ethnic group could be explained through an examination of the ethnic divisions and political persuasion in the officers' coups of the pre-1966 Nigerian Army and the pre-coup relationships between the officers who attempted the coup (Madunagu, 2001). But Ironsi's reactionary counter-coup made this explanation absolutely unattainable.

The killing of top government officials who were from the Northern part of Nigeria by these young military boys did not go down well with their people. Atotarati (2008), submits that most of the coup planners were of Eastern origin, the Northerners saw it as a deliberate plan to eliminate their political elites in order to pave way for the Easterners to take over leadership roles of the country. The aftermaths of the killing resulted in a scale of massacres of people of Eastern Nigeria extraction. There was a total breakdown of law and order in the North and this led to another counter coup which was mainly planned and executed by soldiers from the North. In this counter coup, General Ironsi and many senior military officers from the East were brutally eliminated. The death of General Ironsi (Head of State) created a vacuum in which Lt. Col Gowon a junior officer from the North stepped in to serve the country from disintegration. The new Head of State (now Lt Col Gowon) was a complete gentleman, his integrity and reputation in the army was excellent hence he was readily accepted to the majority of his colleagues, except Col. Ojukwu from the East.

Despite the ascension of Lt Col. Gowon who was from the North, the killing of Igbos and looting of their properties in the North continued unabated. In order to end the senseless killing, Gowon broadcasted to the nation thus: "I receive complaints daily that up till now Easterners (Igbos) living in the north are being killed and molested and their property looted. Therefore, it appears it is going beyond reason and is now at a point of recklessness and irresponsibility" (Atotarati, 2008:3). The ill-treatment muted to the Igbos in the North was out rightly condemned by minority groups in Nigeria. They were of the opinion that if Igbos, who are the third largest group in the country, are treated with disdain and even killed, their existence in Nigeria was in danger. The fear was that they would soon be 'expunged' from Nigeria. This fear is still being expressed to-date by the minorities in Nigeria. One clear example is the Niger Delta, Sango Kataf and Tivs.

The killing of the Igbos and the fact that Lt.Col Gowon was not accepted to be the Head of State by Col. Ojukwu, who was the Governor in the then Eastern region, compelled him to pull the region out from the Nigerian state. On the 30th of May, 1967, Col Ojukwu seceded from Nigeria and named the new nation Biafra. This singular action was resisted by Gowon and this led to the three years civil war (the Biafran War in which over 2 million people from both sides were killed. On June 6, 1969, six months before the war ended, Col Ojukwu and his supporters returned to the communists, radicals and nationalists who were still around and asked them to intervene. An abstract and incoherent manifesto which was commonly known as "the Ahiara Declaration" was hurriedly produced and launched with unprecedented enthusiasm. The peace mission could not be granted since the defeat of the Biafra Republic was eminent. According to Madunagu (2001), it was useless as the whole exercise came rather too late.

The three years' war ended in January 1970. After the war the Nigerian economy which was dependent on agricultural products took a new turn. Crude oil found in the Niger Delta suddenly became the main stay of Nigerian economy (Mngomezulu, 2010). For the victorious Nigerian bourgeoisie and their imperialist collaborators it was a happy re-union. The era of oil money or oil boom brought in high levels of corruption by top officials of Gowon's administration. Kaiser (2005), reports that the combination of corruption, high inflation and poor economic planning limited Gowon's effectiveness and popularity during this tough period. Nigerians were anxious of self-government and almost a decade of military rule coupled with maladministration exhibited by Gowon and his cohorts ensued. His unwillingness to return Nigeria to democratic administration was triggered by the high level of squandermenia of public funds by top government officials. This necessitated General Mohammed to overthrow him and his administration in a coup d'état in 1975, accusing him of clinging on to power against the wishes of the people.

4.4 The Coming of Mohammed/Obasanjo Administration In 1975

Murtala Mohammed's administration acted with despatch and immediately commenced the process of democratizing the country. Within days of ascension into power, he retired all the military men who were said to have embezzled government funds in the past regime. This was immediately followed by massive dismissal of their civilian collaborators in the public service. According to Obi (1999), about more than ten thousand civil servants were compulsorily retired because of corruption and abuse of public office. State house chroniclers and bourgeois story-tellers will like us to forget that radical criticism, patriotic struggle and political heroism almost exclusively provided the grounds for action and created the political and psychological atmosphere in the country which assisted the Murtala group to come to power and consolidate it (Madunagu, 2001).

Mohammed's administration tried not only to reduce the high levels of corruption in Nigeria's polity but put up a spirited effort to reposition the economy which was in shambles through the introduction of different fiscal policies. Mohammed's radicalism and anti-imperialism was not appreciated by a small clique, which was loyal to Gowon. They saw the 'change' as a means of blocking them from enjoying the 'national cake'. Again, this clique was not comfortable with the reform carried out in all sectors; instead, they wanted to remain in office as long as it was possible. In October 1975, Mohammed set the machinery in motion and announced a date for the return of the country to democratic civilian administration on October 1, 1979. This was subsequently followed by the setting up of the Constitution Drafting Committee (CDC) whose main task was to come up with an acceptable constitution for the country.

All these measures to put Nigeria back into the path of glory by General Mohammed did not go down well with a small notorious group of elites and their capitalist allies hence he was assassinated on the 13th February, 1976. By trying to justify their action Mohammed's killers accused him of turning Nigeria into a communist state. A clear example of his popular stand on issues concerning other African countries was his support for the Popular Movement for the Liberation of Angola in the post-independence Angolan civil war. Again, General Mohammed did rebuff President Ford through his fiery speech at the OAU summit in 1976 hence, he was seen by Western capitalists and imperialists as well as African bourgeoisies as a dangerous leader whose presence in the organisation should not only be rejected but expunged. The treatment was equally muted out to Thomas Sankara of Burkina Faso. This date is universally known as lovers' day (Valentine's Day), while the whole world was busy 'pay-rolling' their loved ones, Nigerian peasants, the down-trodden, were busy mourning their bereaved head of state.

After the assassination of Murtala Mohammed, General Obasanjo was persuaded to take over the mantle of leadership in Nigeria. After much persuasion of General Obasanjo by his colleagues in the Nigerian Army, he reluctantly accepted the leadership of the country. General Obasanjo is from the Yoruba ethnic group, the second largest ethnic group in Nigeria and belongs to the Christian religion. Pacheo (1991) argues that in keeping with the chain of command established by his predecessor (Mohammed), Obasanjo pledged to continue with all his programmes, particularly, restoration of democratic civilian government. Again, he carried out a reform in the Nigerian civil service. Obasanjo did not want to perpetuate himself in office because of the nature of how his predecessor was killed; again, Nigerians were tired of military rulers. Furthermore, he was afraid of being toppled by some Northern elements who then dominated the Nigerian army. Possibly, this fear of being overthrown in a coup d'état might have informed his decision to appoint General T.Y. Danjuma and General Shehu Yar'Adua both from the North to the office of Chief of Army Staff and Chief of Staff Supreme respectively.

To fulfil his earlier promise to return the country to civilian rule, Obasanjo threw open the Nigerian political space on September 21, 1978 for active politicking to commence. Within an hour of the lift of ban on political activity, Chief Obafemi Awolowo launched his party called Unity Party of Nigeria (UPN). Other political groups were formed but only five political parties were eventually recognised and registered to partake in the 1979 election. The general election of 1979 was the presidential system which was a complete departure from the 1963 parliamentary system. Kaiser (1991), observes that the adoption of an American presidential system was designed to limit the impact of ethnicity on politics. Obasanjo was of the opinion that the American model would reverse this ugly trend through the separation of power and constitutional provision for checks and balances.

In 1979, the five registered political parties, namely the National Party of Nigeria (NPN), Unity Party of Nigeria (UPN), Great Nigerian Peoples Party (GNPP), Nigerian Peoples Party (NPP) and Peoples Redemption Party (PRP) went into general election in which Shehu Shagari of NPN was declared a winner. To the amazement of Nigerians and some Africans, Obasanjo in keeping with his promise of returning Nigeria to democratic governance handed power over to President Shehu Shagari on October 1, 1979.

4.5 The Consistence and Inconsistence of the Civilian Rule of President Shagari

When President Shagari took over from General Obasanjo, he surrounded himself with notorious politicians whose main aim in office was self-service. From all indications, Shagari meant well for Nigeria, but most of his party men and women were out to plunder the nation's economy through inflation of contracts sums. Some good policies initiated by this government were either not implemented or purposely negatively implemented. A good example is the Green Revolution Programme. Government's intention through the scheme was to cultivate arable land and provide Nigerians with affordable consumable food as well as supply the available industries with raw materials. Millions of dollars were allegedly spent on this project but Ihonvbere (1985), reports that by trying to implement this project about seventy-two per cent of the budgeted sums went into private pockets. To further comatose this project, government went into mass importation of rice and vegetable oil popularly known as *essential commodity* in the political circle.

Another good intention of Shagari's government which was violently abused was the Low Cost Housing Policy (LCHP). The policy in principle made mandatory for government to provide comfortable accommodation for every Nigerian. It is worthy of note that other millions of dollars were equally not only budgeted for the said project but the actual sum was released to contractors who were incidentally Shagari's party members. The "contractors" either absconded with the money leaving the project undone with no consequences or the project was done with total disregard to official government specifications. While his party men and women were busy crippling the Nigerian economy through dubious contract awards, the president himself was busy visiting different countries of the world in the name of trying to create good diplomatic ties with other countries.

In 1982, Shagari's government had to face a serious global economic recession, the price of crude oil which was the main source of revenue to Nigeria dropped. In order to stabilise the economy, different economic measures were put in place. For instance, government had to down-size its workforce. Those who, through god's intervention, survived the mass purse in the civil service were denied promotion for years. While the masses were feeling the pain of the austerity measures, government functionaries were spending the little money meant for physical development and salaries of workers. This fomented a crisis in which government employees experienced months of unpaid salaries. It is pertinent to state that almost all of Shagari's economic resuscitation policies were anti-masses hence his government became unpopular. In other words, the evaporation of Shagari's political legitimacy and acceptability coupled with the undiluted economic doom on the face of his administration were all what the military boys needed to violently overthrow his government. On these grounds, Shagari's government was subsequently toppled by military men led by Brigadier Buhari.

4.6 The Second Coming of the Military Rule in Nigeria

In the early hours of December 30, 1983, three months after President Shagari was sworn in for the second term of four years in a disputed general election which was characterised by violent killings and arson, Brigadier Abacha made the following broadcast to announce the sacking of the second republic:

> Fellow country-men and women, I Brigadier Sani Abacha of the Nigerian Army address you this morning on behalf of the Nigerian Armed Forces. You are all living witnesses to the grave economic predicament and uncertainty which an inept and corrupt leadership has imposed on our beloved nation for the past four years. I am referring to the harsh intolerable condition under which we are living. Our economy has been hopelessly mismanaged. We have become a debtor and beggar nation. There is inadequacy of food at reasonable prices for our people who are now fed up with endless announcements of importation of foodstuff. Health services are in shambles as our hospitals are reduced to mere consulting clinics, without drugs, water equipment. Our educational system is deteriorating at alarming rates. Unemployment figures including the graduates has reached an embarrassing and unacceptable proportion. In some states, workers are being owed salary of 8-12 months. Yet our leaders revel in squander mania and corruption, and indiscipline continues to proliferate public appointments in complete disregard of our stark economic realities. After due consideration over these deplorable conditions, I and my colleagues in the armed forces have, in the discharge of our national role as the promoters and protectors of national interests decided to effect a change in the

government of the Federal Republic of Nigeria to form a Federal Military Government. This task has just been completed.

From the tune of the text, it was obvious that military boys and their civilian allies presented themselves as the alternative political party whose main duty was to create, maintain and sustain law, order and discipline in Nigeria. Brigadier Buhari's regime tried to resuscitate the nation's economy through various economic policies. The corrupt politicians were tried in the different tribunals set up to recover embezzled funds. As the Buhari administration tried to stabilise the country socially, politically and economically, his colleagues in the military did not like his style of leadership which was more of a 'strict fiscal discipline' hence he was edged out of office by Ibrahim Babangida. The reason given by Babangida and his boys for toppling Buhari's regime was that he was autocratic in his style of leadership. There is general consensus in the academy that the reason given from all indications is not only infantile in conception but porous in its delivery because it was clear from the onset that Babangida and his lieutenants were only using the excuse to edge out his boss so that he could ascend to power.

4.7 Ibrahim Babangida and His Endless Transition

It would be fair to say that Babangida initiated the 'president for life' syndrome in Nigeria. On August 27, 1985, President Babangida (first military head of state to declare himself president) came into power. His antics of hanging on to power were dubious in character and satanic in form hence, he was nicknamed Maradona (the great Argentinian player). His first task was to declare a National Economic Emergency (NEE) and engaged Nigerians to debate on the option to either accept the IMF loan and the conditions attached to it or to embark on more austere economic measures that would require great sacrifices. One year and eight months was given to Nigerians to debate on this and at the end of it all, Babangida declined the IMF loan but rather opted for the Structural Adjustment Programme (SAP). According to Nnwu (1992), SAP was designed to fit the standard IMF -World Bank structural adjustment package. The scholar observes that SAP was meant to effectively alter and restructure the consumption and production patterns of the Nigerian economy and eliminate price distortion and heavy dependence on the export of crude oil and import of consumer and producer goods. The implementation of SAP is still being felt today in Nigeria because the programme - instead of alleviating poverty among Nigerians - impoverished them even more.

The second trick used by Babangida to perpetuate himself in office was the setting up of the Political Bureau with the following terms of reference:

(a) Review Nigeria's political history and identify the basic problems which have led to our failure in the past and suggest ways of resolving and coping with these problems.

(b) Identify a basic philosophy of government which will determine goals and serve as a guide to the activities of government.

(c) Collect relevant information and data for the government as well as identify other political problems that may arise from the debate.

(d) Gather, collate and evaluate the contributions of Nigerians to the search for a viable political and provide guides for the attainment of the consensus objective

(e) Deliberate on the other political problems as may be referred to it from time to time.

They met for a period of 15 months and then recommended a transition period starting from 1987 and ending by 1990. But government, in its views on the Report, rejected the 1990 terminal date and rather opted for 1992 as the year the military would relinquish power. The Bureau, in addition, called for the setting up of a small size constitutional review panel to produce the draft of the amended version of the presidential system of government.

The Bureau, however, asked for a Referendum on the Draft Constitution to be so produced. According to Madunagu (2001), the government not only rejected this recommendation it also threw out the Bureau's socialism; not a "utopian" socialism or petty-bourgeois socialism, but a form of socialism which was characterised by a radical shift in the balance of class power.

President Babangida constituted the CDC whose major duty was to come up with an acceptable Constitution for the Third Republic. After exhaustive deliberation, the CDC came out with what one would regard as 'near people's Constitution' but the president in his normal 'maradonna style' rejected a greater part of the clauses. The aftermath of this action was that the 1989 Constitution which was promulgated in May of 1989 had nothing in common with the Bureau's report and recommendations.

On May 3, 1989, Babangida lifted the ban on political activities, Nigerians were asked to form political parties and equally seek for their registration. At the end of the day, about seventeen political parties were formed and applied for registration. It is pertinent to state that in order for Babangida to hang on to power, he rejected all political groups that were formed by Nigerians, instead, came up with two government parties which were Social Democratic Party (SDP) and National Republican Convention (NRC). His reason for the rejection of political groups was that they had ethnic colouration. However, it was only in Nigeria that government formed political parties and went ahead to fund them for her citizens. This record still remains unbroken to-date.

Another crude way which President Babangida used to perpetuate himself in office was the ban of old politicians in the Nigerian political arena. He used unrefined laws to ban politicians he perceived as a hindrance to his mission. His action for many Nigerians was not surprising because in October 1988, three years after seizing power and well into the political transition he inaugurated, he declared that although he did not know who would succeed him, he knew who would not. After he had exhausted all the antics to hang on to power, the stage was finally set for the general election. The two presidential candidates (Chief MKO Abiola of the SDP and Alhaji O. B. Torfa of the NRC) went into the election on June 12, 1993. The election was declared by local and international observers as the freest and fairest in the history of Nigeria.

As the National Electoral Commission (NEC) - an umbrella body saddled with the responsibility of conducting the election - started declaring the result of the presidential election, President Babangida, in order to remain in power against the will and wishes of Nigerians arrested the results through a questionable court judgement. The court judgement stopping further release of the election results was obtained by a faceless organisation known as the Association for Better Nigeria (ABN), despite the fact that there was an existing law that outlawed any court in Nigeria from stopping the presidential election either from holding or releasing results.

On June 23, 1993, an unsigned statement from the presidency announced the annulment of this most popular election ever conducted in the history. Three days later, General Babangida made a radio and television broadcast in which he officially annulled the election. The reason given for the annulment was that the said election was characterised by high levels of corruption. He did not only annul the election but went further to ban the two presidential candidates and also dissolved the National Electoral Commission. The emerging drama instituted by Babangida put the country into a serious crisis in which many Nigerians were killed. Edaozie (2002), reports that, many Nigerians across the country from different sectors of society (including those in the cities, the business sector and those from Abiola's home area in the west) took to the streets in protest. These protests further debilitated an already fragile economy. When General Babangida realised that his mission of staying in power could not be attained, he established the Interim National Government headed by Chief Ernest Shonekan and handed power to him. This finally brought to an end Babangida's administration in which within his eight years of misrule he witnessed high levels of the killing of political opponents, including Dele Giwa who was killed through a parcel bomb. Madunagu (2001) held that Babangida's regime witnessed some of the worst riots, strikes and mass protests in the nation's history than any leader before him.

4.8 The Most Deadly Of Them All

According to Suberu (1999), the sense of anguish evoked by the Third Republic's collapse should not detract us from the positive element of the post-element crisis that culminated in Abacha's coup. The first was the apparent humiliation and ultimate defect of Babangida's extraordinary manipulative and cynical dictatorship by a disparate coalition of forces within and outside of the sectarian tensions inflamed by the wanton annulment of the victory of the first southerner to be elected head of government in the nation's thirty four year-old history. On November 17, 1993, General Sani Abacha overthrew Chief Ernest Shonekan who spent only four months in office. The latter established Provisional Ruling Council (PRC) with himself as chairman and General Diya, as vice chairman. Young and Beckett (1997), assert that Abacha's years of military rule were no different from many of his predecessors, in terms of using force to severely curtain oppositions.

On his ascension to power, Abacha immediately commenced the process of elongating his stay in office by dismantling all the democratic structures which were put in place by Babangida. For instance, he dissolved the two political parties, the National and States Assembly and the Electoral body. He appointed prominent members of the political class into his government. Among the political class so appointed was Chief MKO Abiola's running mate (Baba Gana Kingibe) in the annulled June 12, 1993 election. This politician was then an executive member of the SDP at the local government level. One could view the action of Baba Gana Kingibe as the highest level of betrayal. An activist and Lawyer in the person of Chief Nwankwo put it thus: "It was the biggest shock of my life. We took risk in the name of democracy. Hundreds were killed by the National Guard. Hundreds were detained by SSS and the police. Then our so called pro-democracy leaders joined the military to terminate democracy. I cannot believe it". Similarly, Babarinsa (1993), observes that it is part of the tragedy of Nigeria that when the military decided to intervene finally, it did not do so on the side of the electorates, instead, it sided with those who voided the June 12, verdict. It sided with the anti-democratic cabals who had been holding the nation hostage for more than three decades. Abiola was later arrested and detained for declaring himself president by Abacha who started manhunt of opposition groups.

In his bid to hang on to power, General Abacha set up deadly killer squads known as *strike force* and *body guard* whose duty was to eliminate any person or group who stood between him and his mission. For instance, Kudirat Abiola (wife of MKO Abiola), Pa Rewane, Ken Saro-Wiwa and other pro-democratic members were all murdered. Activists such as Wole Soyinka, Prince Fayemi, Chief Bola Tinubu, among others went on self-exile to avoid being killed. The media houses that tried to oppose his elongation bid were either closed down or set ablaze. It was during this 'dark era' that most journalists were sent to prison. General Abacha did not only use force to perpetuate himself in office, he also used public funds to bribe a greater number of his supporters. Former President Obasanjo reported in one of his public functions that General Abacha manipulated and abused the press; he relied on the politics of settlement to get support, and inconsistent, changing statements and policies like the weathercock. Again, his undiluted appetite for money catapulted him to an enviable position of the most corrupt Nigerian leader.

General Abacha set up a Constitutional Conference to determine the way forward for Nigeria politically. He did not give Nigerians a date for his disengagement from office, rather he made every Nigerian to believe that his exist date would be determined by the members of the conference. At the end of it all, the Constitutional Conference members, due to military pressure and monetary inducement from the presidency, gave him no particular date for his disengagement from office but rather said that he could leave office after fixing all Nigerian problems. The question in the mind of patriotic Nigerians was how one individual could be able to fix all of the country's problems. Indirectly, the members were giving him a licence he was looking for to remain in power almost indefinitely.

General Abacha was absolutely obsessed with power to the extent that the Nigerian economy was left in the hands of his Minister of Finance. Ihonvbere (1996) submits that Abacha's budgets were not based on any serious appreciation of the nation's economic realities and predicaments. It was during this period that unemployment, armed robbery, prostitutes smuggling, youth restiveness, among others were at their peak in the country. Despite all these vices and the collapse of many infrastructures in the country, Abacha's bank accounts continued to swell on a daily basis. The Federal Government of Nigeria estimated that Abacha looted four billion dollars from the nation's treasury. Similarly, *The Times* of London held that a total sum of money siphoned by Abacha from Nigeria was $6.6 billion.

Abacha's resolve to stay in power indefinitely was not in doubt. This was evidenced on the political structures he put on the ground to actualise his dream. Firstly, the five political parties approved and registered for the general election all adopted him as their presidential candidate. Secondly, he single-handedly picked the chairman of the National Electoral Commission of Nigeria (NECON) and saddled him with the responsibility of conducting the general election. Thirdly, he intimidated any credible candidate wanting to challenge him on the presidential race. Whilst still laying the foundation to actualise his dream of being the life president of Nigeria, he died mysteriously. Whether this was a blessing or a curse for Nigeria remains debatable.

4.9 Blind Abdulsalami Abubakar's Political Transition

With the death of General Abacha, his political structures put in place to ensure that he remained in power for life were violently dismantled by his lieutenants. The new head of state in person of General A. Abubakar immediately opened the prison gates and set free all the activists who were wrongfully sent to jail or detained by Abacha. From all indications, he refused to release Chief MKO Abiola who won the annulled June 12 election. Abiola finally died in detention while taking tea in the presence of the US delegation that had come to negotiate his release. The question is why was Abiola not released with other pro-democratic activists? Nigerians say Abubakar has some questions to answer in this direction.

Within few weeks of Abubakar's ascension to power, the 1999 Constitution was promulgated and three political parties were registered, namely: Alliance for Democracy (AD), All Peoples Party (APP) and Peoples Democratic Party (PDP). These three registered political parties were formed by Chief Bola Ige and their manifestoes solely written by him. Therefore, to this date there are no noticeable and significant differences in the context of the manifestoes of the parties. It was on this strength that Enemuo (1999) submits that with no significant ideological differences, the parties were agglomerations of Nigeria's notables, individuals who have been prominent in past civilian and military regimes and business, as well as a handful of young wealthy professionals and businessmen.

Abubakar was not ready to resolve any political and economic mess created by his predecessors hence, his hasty announcement of political programmes. Because of the nature of how the transition programme was hurriedly planned, credible candidates were unable to come out and contest for elective positions. Again, the cabals from the northern part of Nigeria wanted a stooge from the south whom they could control to be president hence, they handpicked former general Obasanjo who was serving life jail term. Commentators argue that since they actually wanted to impose Obasanjo on the generality of Nigeria the election conducted was a charade.

There was a strong indication that before the 1999 general election was conducted the winner was known already. This position was based on the utterances by one of the key figures from the North and who eventually held an important political office in Obasanjo's government that if their candidate (Obasanjo) did not win he would go on self-exile. From the political perspective, Abubakar's transition was as much an attempt at securing the survival of the military as a national institution, as it was an act of self-preservation through the protection of the military faction of the Nigerian political class, which was clearly threatened by Abacha's self-succession plan as well as the revolutionary pressure emanating from sections of civil society (Obi, 2000).

4.10 Obasanjo's Transition and His Tall Dreams

Before President Obasanjo ascended to power for the second time on May 29, 1999, he promised Nigerians that he would step on toes. Immediately after his assumption of power, Obasanjo retired all military men and women who held political appointments in the country. His decision to compulsorily send those 'national treasury looters' to retirement were applauded by Nigerians. Again, he set up a panel to look into different contracts awarded by the military regimes from 1983 to 1999. Similarly, a panel (Oputa panel) was constituted to investigate all human rights abuses that were perpetuated by the military. In the views of Obi (2000), a lot was done in the area of the decompression of authoritarianism in Nigeria. These positive moves were subsequently applauded by ordinary Nigerians, suddenly the 'music' changed and the 'dance steps' equally reflected a new rhythm.

President Obasanjo's new dance steps were invariably decided by those cabals who initiated his ascension to power in the first instance. It is worthy of mention that different recommendations from the panels were summarily swept under the carpet, because most of these recommendations directly affected the majority of those who brought him out of prison and subsequently elected him to be the president of Nigeria. After the expiration of the grace period, Obasanjo began to exhibit his raw and crude power on Nigerians through different economic policies. For instance, prices of petroleum products were increased arbitrarily, public industries, buildings and institutions were sold to his friends at the amount far below the prevailing market price, and this was a clear case of open state robbery. In another development, Obasanjo's hatred to some ethnic nationalities in the country that either criticised or opposed some of his actions and decisions were dealt with accordingly in various ways. For example, he, in commando style, ordered the destruction of Tivland in Benue state and Odi land in Bayelsa state, among others. His opposition to the Niger Delta region course of resource control was evident on the impeachment and detention of a sitting state governor of Bayelsa state who was the arrow head in the resource control agitations.

President Obasanjo's abuse of the Constitution was reflected in his non adherence to the principles of separation of power which is enshrined in the 1999 Nigerian Constitution. Throughout the eight years of his administration, Obasanjo decided who sat as the senate president and speaker of the House of Representatives. Towards the tail end of his second term in office, Obasanjo in the characteristic manner of African dictators attempted to annul the constitution and re-write it to perpetuate himself in office. This attempt which is popularly called 'Third term agenda' was shot down by the different progressive forces in Nigeria. The eventual killing of his tenure elongation bid compelled him to draft the late President Alhaji Umaru Yar'Adua into the presidential race to ensure his soft landing. Obasanjo forced other presidential hopefuls in person of Chief Victor Atta, Chief Odili, Chief Donald Duke, among others to step down for Yar'Adua. He succeeded. But Yar'Adua was evidently sick and some predicted that he would not stay long in office. Indeed, this is what happened. Goodluck Jonathan, his deputy, assumed power as per the dictates of the National Constitution. Only time will tell if Jonathan will deviate from the norm.

4.11 Implications of Years of Misrule in Nigeria

Misrule in Nigeria has had long-lasting negative effects in various spheres of life. For example, the introduction of formal education into Nigeria can be seen as a principal catalyst that has shaped her socio-economic system. At various historical epochs, education has directly or indirectly occupied the centre stage of economic, social and political events in the country. With the frequent military interventions in the Nigerian political landscape, the hitherto functional education system was defaced and its products regarded as unproductive.

Nigeria inherited the British system of education on attainment of independence. The 6-5-2-3 system adapted (i.e. 6 years primary, 5 years secondary, 2 years higher school and 3 years tertiary education) from Britain mainly focused on the cognitive domain, ignoring affective and psychomotor domains. To embrace all the three domains of learning and the integration of indigenous knowledge into the curriculum, government set up the National Curriculum Conference in 1969. The purpose of the conference was to review old and identify new national goals for Nigerian education, bearing in mind the needs of the youths and adults in the task of nation-building and national reconstruction for social and economic well-being of the individual and the society (Fafunwa, 1989). At the end of the conference, far reaching recommendations were made. Prominent among those recommendations were the institutionalisation of the National Policy on Education whose guiding principles are: the desire that Nigeria should be a free, just and democratic society, a land full of opportunities for all its citizens, able to generate a great and dynamic economy, and growing into a united, strong and self-reliant nation. The document went further to highlight the national aims and objectives to which the philosophy is linked such as the inculcation of national consciousness and national unity.

The conference equally recommended the abandonment of the British system of education and the adoption of the 6-3-3-4 system of education. Various educational bodies were involved in the planning for the smooth take-off of the proposed new educational system in the country. The new educational system from the onset suffered poor implementation because of political interference. For instance, during Babangida's regime the education policy that transferred the management of primary education to local council from the states was enacted. Teachers were recruited and their salaries not paid for months. Consequently, most qualified teachers abandoned the teaching profession and took other jobs. There was total neglect of all education sectors during Babangida's administration. This is the void Obasanjo wanted to fill.

The situation was not better during Abacha's regime, secondary and university education were starved of funds. Strikes by lecturers and non-academic staff were common occurrence, in some instances universities were closed up to twelve months. There was serious 'brain drain' in the country; most renowned academics were forced to relocate to other countries in Africa, Europe and America. Academic freedom was curtailed and few academics who decided to remain in the country were often monitored by security operatives and more often than not were arrested on the order of the president. There was a general insecurity in the university environment.

The education sector during the second coming of Obasanjo did not better after all, the Universal Basic Education programme introduced by him could not see the light of the day because of high levels of corruption perpetuated by his ministers. In 2001, Obasanjo's administration allocated little above six present of that year's budget to the education sector while the presidency got more than twelve present. The long years of neglect of the education sector by different military administrations in Nigeria impacted negatively on the quality of the graduates the country's universities produced. Most of the young graduates were 'half baked'. This position was supported by one time Governor of the Central Bank of Nigeria when he said that seventy five present of Nigerian graduates were unemployable. This is an indication of the level of destruction experienced in the education sector by Nigerians as a result of leaders who imposed themselves on the electorate and used brute force to sustain themselves. Such negative effects were witnessed in other spheres of life but time and space will not allow that discussion to be included in this chapter. Such is food for thought.

4.12 Conclusion

By all accounts, the Nigerian case study is a sad story. No country in Africa has had as many military governments as Nigeria. Noticeably, almost all the military rulers assumed power under false pretence. They claimed to be representing the wishes of the electorate. Meanwhile, they oppressed the very people they claimed to represent. With no exception, the strategies they used were: force and bribery. The latter came in two forms. First, those who supported the incumbent presidents were given high positions in government regardless of their credentials and capabilities or expertise. Second, supporters were showered with money looted from state coffers. With regards to the former method of sustaining themselves in office (the use of force) leaders use state institutions to silence potential opposition. This strategy is a common feature in African politics as the other case studies discussed in this manuscript show.

In discussing the reigns of the various military and few civilian rulers in Nigeria this chapter has demonstrated that political avarice, egotism and economic greed were the characteristic features of these leaders. But another point worth noting is that without exception, these leaders resorted to the survival means outlined above because they knew that they were not the best candidates for the position(s) they occupied. Also, they were mindful of the fact that they did not enjoy the support of the masses. The carrot and stick mechanisms were used interchangeably pending the situation at the time. In both instances, the incumbent presidents succeeded in prolonging their stay in office.

Lastly, this chapter has shown that the obsession with power and all the bad practices which accompanied it had detrimental effects in the life spheres of Nigerians. The economy declined, the education system deteriorated, open political engagement was suppressed thus limiting any chance for innovation and demonstration of political wisdom. Most importantly, the political, social, and economic environment forced a number of academics to leave the country. Those who remained in the country had to tread cautiously because the intelligence operatives were keeping an open eye on them. The same autocratic leaders later started complaining about brain drain, forgetting that they were the ones promoting it. Similar trends can be found in countries such as Kenya where Moi's government started to purge potential academics and forced a number of them out of the country to avoid being killed. As demonstrated in this chapter, successive Nigerian leaders got obsessed with power and did all in their power to sustain their stay in office. As in the other case studies discussed in this book, the actions by Nigeria's leaders give Nigeria a license to be called one of the promoters of the 'president for life' phenomenon.

References

Akinterinwa, B. A. (2005). (Ed.) *Nigeria and the Development of the African Union*. Ibadan: Vantage Publishers.

Anwu, J. (1992). "President Babangida's Structural Adjustment Programme and Inflation in Nigeria". *Journal of Social Development in Africa*. 7 (1) 5-24.

Bassey, M. O (1999). *Western Education and Political Domination in Africa: A Study in Critical and Dialogical Pedagogy.* Westport: Bergin & Garvey.

Babarinsa, B. (1993). "The new inheritance". Tell Magazine. Lagos.

Chabal, P. (1994). *Power in Africa: An Essay in Political Interpretation.* New York: St. Martin Press.

Enemuo, J. (1999). "Elite solidarity, communal support and the 1999 Presidential Election in Nigeria". *Journal of Opinion.* XXVII/1.

Fafunwa, A. B. (1985). *National Policy on Education: A Planner's Viewpoint,* in Tamuno, T N and Atanda, J A. (eds.) *Nigeria Since Independence: The First 25 Years.* Ibadan: Heinemann Education Books Ltd.

Garba, J. (1987). *Diplomatic Soldiering.* Ibadan: Spectrum Books.

Ihonvbere, J O (1996). "Are things falling apart? The military and the crisis of democratisation in Nigeria". *The Journal of Modern African Studies.* 34 (2). 193-225.

Madunagu, E (2001). *The Making and Unmaking of Nigeria: Critical Essay on Nigerian History and Politics.* Calabar: Clear Lines Publications.

Mngomezulu, B. R. (2010). "Economic inequalities and the Niger Delta crisis in Nigeria: Challenges and prospects". Paper presented at the International Conference on Territorial Origins of African Civil Conflicts, University of Kwa-Zulu Natal, 29-30 January.

Obi, C (2000). "Last Card: Can Nigeria survive another political transition?" *African Journal of Political Science.* 5 (2) 67-86.

Obiyan, S (1999). "Political Parties under the Abubakar transition programme and democratic stability in Nigeria". *Journal of Opinion* 27 (1) 41-43.

Ogbondah, C.W (2000). "Political Repression in Nigeria, 1993-98: A critical examination of one aspect of the perils of military dictatorship". *African Spectrum.* 35 (2) 231-242.

Osokoya, I O (1986). *6-3-3-4 Education in Nigeria: History, Strategies, Issues and Problems.* Ibadan: Laurel Educational Publishers.

Subaru, R (1999). "Integration and disintegration in the Nigerian federation", in D. Bach (ed.), *Regionalisation in Nigeria: Integration and Disintegration.* Oxford: James Currey and Indiana University Press.

Udogu, E. I. (2005). (ed.) *Nigeria in the Twenty-First Century*. Eritrea: Africa World Press.

CHAPTER 5: ZAMBIA

Frederick Chiluba's Tactics Used to Sustain His Stay in Power

Bhekithemba Richard Mngomezulu

THE MAP OF ZAMBIA

5.1 Introduction

Zambia is arguably one of those African countries with a potential to do well economically given the fact that it has various natural mineral resources which could attract foreign currency, more especially copper. But for some reason, the country is not at the level where it should be economically. This is mainly due to human factors. As a point of departure, it is worth noting that the political experience in Zambia is slightly different from that of Kenya, Zimbabwe and Nigeria in many respects. In the case of Kenya, for example, the first two presidents ruled the country for more than two decades each (President Kenyatta, 1963-1978 and President Moi, 1978-2002) and would have stayed in office for much longer were it not for the cause of nature (in the case of President Kenyatta) or the loss of patience by opposition parties (in the case of President Moi). With regards to Zambia, it was only the founding President, Kenneth Kaunda, who ruled the country for more than two decades as shall be seen below. His successors were bound by the constitution to remain in office for a specified maximum period and leave. Where an incumbent president tried to prolong his stay in power, the Zambian leadership in government scuttled such plans thus forcing the president to quit when his constitutional mandate had expired.

But it is interesting to note that despite having been in office for over two decades and having control over various state institutions, President Kaunda did not loot the state like the other leaders discussed in this book. By the time he went to his retirement in 1991, President Kaunda only had the equivalent of $8, 000 in his bank account as opposed to the billions of dollars other African leaders boasted about when they left the highest political office. Moreover, Kaunda had no house of his own, nor did he have business or assets and investments either in Zambia or abroad. This was a stark difference from most African leaders, including his successor, Frederick Chiluba, as discussed later in this chapter. It is in this context that Kaunda is viewed as "a man of great personal integrity and parsimony", someone whose economic dealings and policies "generally did not exhibit self-interest" (Mills, 2010:205). To this day, Kaunda is still regarded as one of the few African leaders who did not allow power to corrupt them and tarnish their public image as is the case with leaders like

Mobutu Sese Seko of the then Zaire who was richer than the country he ruled.

This chapter takes a brief look at the history of Zambia from pre-colonial times when Africans were living on their own, discusses the colonial period and Britain's attempts to force the country into a federation with other neighbouring territories, and then proceeds to address postcolonial politics in Zambia when Africans were in charge of their affairs once again. Most importantly, and of relevance to the theme of this book, the chapter provides a detailed analysis of President Frederick Chiluba's false pretences and cunning ways aimed at elongating his stay in power in order to satisfy his financial needs. An attempt is also made in this chapter to draw similarities between President Chiluba's actions on the one hand, and those of leaders such as President Daniel arap Moi in Kenya, President Olusegun Obasanjo in Nigeria as well as Presidents Hastings Kamuzu Banda and Bakili Muluzi in Malawi. Through these comparisons, the aim is to see how Zambia fits in the broader scheme of things.

5.2 A Brief History of Zambia and the Review of the Literature

Zambia, as shown in the map above, shares the geographical borders with Angola, Zimbabwe, Mozambique, Malawi and Tanzania. It is in this context that Grotpeter (1998) describes this country as the link between the independent states of Central, East and West Africa, as well as the Southern African region in general. In other words, although Zambia is away from the seas, it is strategically located and has access to different regions on the African continent. In the past, farmers from the north-eastern part of present-day Zambia "practiced *citamene*, a system of shifting agriculture that required large tracts of land but maximized scarce soil nutrients" (McCann, 1999: 17). Archaeological evidence shows that pre-colonial Zambia used cowrie shells and pottery. During the colonial era, there is evidence that a significant number of Zambians (more than a third of the population, to be exact) embraced Christianity as a religion. After independence in 1964, the government faced opposition from churches established much earlier, such as the Lumpa church (Fage, 1986). It is pertinent, therefore to begin by tracing the history of this country and have a better understanding of the phases it went through. It is through this exercise that we can glean the sources of some of the practices witnessed at a much later period by the political leadership.

The people of Zambia are the Bantu speaking people who, in c1000 settled in the region that is called Zambia today. They migrated from the North to the South as most other Bantu groups who moved in the same direction and subsequently populated or inhabited a hostile environment (Iliffe, 1998). The Shona people arrived in the area c1100 and saw that the once empty region was now gradually populated by these communities. In 1300 the Mwene Mutapa Empire was established in the region. It included the Southern part of what is now called Zambia, Zimbabwe and Mozambique. These migrations and settlements were followed by the arrival of the Luba and Lunda people in the region. It should be noted that there were no white people at this stage. It was not until 1796 that the first white explorer arrived here from Mozambique by crossing the Luangwa River. But unlike the colonialists who followed a few years later, he was not a harmful person or someone with bad intentions. He came here simply to carry on with his exploration work which was driven by the desire to know more about the world - including Africa - and nothing else. By contrast, the other whites who arrived in the nineteenth century came with the intention to occupy and rule.

The Zulu king, King Shaka, contributed to the diversification of the population of this region through his intermittent wars with his neighbours and some kings from afar. Through these wars generally referred to as the *mfecane* or *difaqane*, which literally means the crushing. King Shaka wanted to extend the Zulu Kingdom and protect it by having many kings who paid allegiance to him even if they were far from his royal residence. Part of the reason for these wars was the disastrous effect of major drought which led to *Madlathule* (the one who eats while remaining quiet). King Shaka was feared and respected at the same time. Those who could not face him resorted to running away with some of their followers. That is how the group of Nguni people called Makololo found its way to present-day Zambia in 1835. Others ended up in present-day Tanzania in East Africa. Thus, it is not an exaggeration to state that the so-called *mfecane* wars, or the crushing as some would say, turned the whole southern Africa upside down (Bureau of African Affairs, 11 April 2011; see also http://www. Africanhistory.about.com/od/Zambia/I/B1-Zambia-Timeline.htm).

But as much as it is true that King Shaka played a major role in these wars of territorial expansion, some scholars argue that it would be erroneous to give agency solely to him as an individual. They argue that the wars were a product of the struggles between all the emergent rival states north of the Thukela River. In fact, polities such as the Ngwane, Bhaca, Sotho Ndebele/Khumalo and Mpondo are sometimes associated with the mfecane. Debates around this concept are endless and it is not the intention of this chapter to dwell on them because that is not the focus of the current manuscript. There are authors who have addressed the issue in different contexts (Wylie, 2006; Hamilton, 1998; Laband, 1997; Hamilton, 1995; Cobbing, 1988; Omer-Cooper, 1966; Walker, 1928).

Historians, anthropologists, and archaeologists have continued to document the history of Zambia, paying emphasis on different times, themes and kingdoms or chiefdoms. Roberts (1976), used evidence from archaeology, anthropology, oral traditions and written sources to document the history of Zambia. In his work, Roberts provides a compelling discussion on the rise of chieftainship in Zambia as well as the expansion of trade, patterns of settlement, as well as production starting from the early Iron Age. He uses linguistic evidence to demonstrate both the similarities and differences between a variety of languages. Moreover, he discusses different religious beliefs followed by different communities in pre-colonial Zambia. Most importantly, he addresses the issue of social institutions which pre-date colonialism and makes the point that these were part and parcel of pre-colonial chiefdoms and kingdoms, not only in what would later become Zambia, but also in Southern Africa in general. Drawing from some published sources, Roberts touches on different important themes in the entire Savannah region of Central Africa which cover various aspects of life. This complements Iliffe's discussion of African history and his notion that Britain occupied Northern Rhodesia (Zambia) and Nyasaland (Malawi) defying Portugal's claims (Iliffe, 1995). Roberts concludes his book by highlighting some of the many problems that were experienced by the independent state of Zambia since it obtained its political independence from Britain in 1964.

Phiri's recent work entitled *A political history of Zambia* (2011) focuses primarily on the period after independence. His work is an examination of the introduction of the one-party state in Zambia as well as its role in the political history of the country. In this work, Phiri advances the view that the failure of multi-party politics in Zambia during the First Republic (1964-1972) was a clear reflection of lack of preparedness of the body politic during the colonial times to put systems in place for plural politics post the colonial era. Inferred in this argument is the view that Zambians obtained independence having not fully prepared for it. However, he concedes that the political leadership amassed skills and knowledge over time and looked beyond national boundaries for lessons. He is of the view that the re-introduction of multi-party politics in 1990 (ending the long rule of President Kenneth Kaunda) came as a result of both endogenous and exogenous causal factors. Among influential international developments he cites the collapse of communist regimes in Eastern Europe and argues that this made communism dispensable in African politics.

But even after embracing multi-party democracy, Phiri insists that Zambians still struggled to find a tight grip on procedures characterizing a democratic dispensation. Thus, he opines that when Zambia held the third multi-party elections in 2001 there were still evident serious doubts regarding the future of the entire democratic project being experimented in the country. Phiri then embarks on a very critical appraisal of the one-party participatory democracy which was introduced in Zambia after independence. He is of the strong view that both the problems and experiences of plural politics in the Third Republic were by and large a reflection of the weakness of the opposition political parties as well as the intransigence of the political party in power at the time. He concludes by stating that the Movement for Multiparty Democracy (MMD) enjoys the status of *a defecto* one-party monopoly which derives influence from the one-party regime of the 1960s (Phiri, 2011).

Certain scholars who write about the history of Zambia tend to focus primarily on specific chiefdoms and kingdoms in their investigation and do not paint a broader picture about Zambia as a country. For example, Saha (1994), writes about the history of the Tonga chiefs and their people who inhabit the Monze District. He addresses their different aspects of life in great detail. Macola (2003), provides a detailed account of the history of the Kingdom of Kazembe in North-eastern Zambia, including Katanga. He covers the period from the formation of this Kingdom right up to 1950. Kazembe is known as the largest of central Africa's Lunda Kingdoms. This Kingdom is said to have been established in the 1740s and remained until 1890. Throughout this period it was ruled by no less than 9 kings in total.

In terms of the chronology in Zambia's historiography, Herbert's *Twilight on the Zambezi* (2002), deals with late colonialism in Central Africa. He discusses the characteristic features of this geographical space during the period in question. He begins by discussing the history of Zambia when it was still known as Northern Rhodesia. He then discusses the views of the native councils, colonial leaders, campaigners of independence and the British Colonial Office in London. This provides a balanced account of how each of these constituencies felt about the pending independence. Contrary to the general tendency to perceive African colonies as being homogeneous entities, Herbert addresses the complexities of decolonization in Africa and demonstrates the heterogeneous nature of these colonies. With specific reference to Zambia, for example, he focuses on the year 1959, the year before the beginning of the events that would culminate in the independence of Zambia. This is an important contribution to the historiography of Zambia. As discussed above, authors such as Phiri take the discussion forward and cover the period after independence. This is the period discussed in the manuscript during which the 'president for life' syndrome presented itself at different moments as discussed later in the present chapter.

Zambia is known in history as a copper producing country. This was one of the major causes of the colonization of this region, although not the only one. As a result of colonial policies in Africa, "African economies thus became export-oriented, largely dependent on a single product (rubber for Liberia, cocoa for the Gold Coast, peanuts for Senegal, copper for Zambia and Katanga, etc.), with ultimate dependence on colonial power" (Harris, 1998:228). Zambia, like other African colonies, was drawn into this one product economy. In 1920 word spread around that tons of copper had been found in present-day Zambia, more particularly at a place called Broken Hill. Subsequent to this discovery more and more Europeans flocked into the area to try their luck as they did with the discovery of coal and gold in present-day South Africa. Suffice to say that by this time the Scramble for Africa was well under way. It was only being intensified. For example, in 1951 the Conservative government in Britain embraced the idea of establishing a Federation. Indeed, this federation, called the Central African Federation (CAF), was formed in August 1953 and Britain forced Zambia to join it. Besides Zambia, the Federation included southern Rhodesia (present-day Zimbabwe) and Nyasaland (present-day Malawi). The aim was to bring these countries together for easy administration.

The federation was formed along the lines of the East African Community during its infant stages before East Africans embraced the idea but resolved to form the federation on their terms (Mngomezulu, 2009; Mngomezulu, 2004a; Mngomezulu, 2004b; Mngomezulu, 2003). While it is true that the 1920, copper discovery in Zambia invited more Europeans to the region as noted above, it should not be misconstrued as the spark which ignited to trigger the colonization of these African people as this had already started years back.

As more and more Europeans settled in this region, the local people could not tolerate them. In response, the locals expressed their resentment to the manner in which Europeans were treating them. The Northern Rhodesian African Congress Party (NRACP), established in 1948, lost popular support when it failed to prevent the inauguration of the Central African Federation. However, the Zambian political leadership was determined to rid their country of British domination or hegemony. During the early 1950s, Zambian politicians such as Kenneth Kaunda (affectionately known to his compatriots as cde KK), Harry Nkumbula, Simon Kapwepwe and a few others were already assiduously planning for a free Zambia. They were dubbed 'rebels'. Some of these so-called rebels were immediately incarcerated for their actions.

In 1958, Kaunda, Kapwepwe and other Zambian politicians formed the Zambian African National Congress (ZANC). This followed their split with Nkumbula who was seen at the time as a moderate politician. In 1959, ZANC was banned and Kaunda and other leaders were summarily put behind bars for their political activities which did not impress the British administration as well as the colonial government and its authorities in the area. They were suspected of planning to kill whites in the country. As a general norm, the architects of colonialism and respective decision-makers in each of the African countries or colonies hoped that the use of brute force would dampen the spirit of those who defied colonial rule. Unfortunately, in Zambia, as in many other African colonies, this never happened. Eventually, in 1960, Kaunda and his comrades were released from jail.

Once free men, they formed what they called the United National Independence Party (UNIP) in 1960 and elected Kaunda as its president. The party was banned the following year. But it is worth noting that these early formations had ways to resurrect and fight back with oomph. One of the aims of the UNIP was to disband the federation. This was in line with a recommendation made by a Commission led by Lord Monckton that each territory had to be allowed to secede from the federation if it wanted to do so (Oliver, 1990). Indeed this dream became a reality when the Central African Federation was eventually dissolved in 1963. In a way, this marked a great triumph of the African people. After many years of struggle, Zambia was on its way to freedom. In 1962, Nkumbula joined Kaunda in a coalition. In 1964, Kaunda won the elections and became the first Prime Minister. On 24 October, 1964, Zambia obtained full independence from Britain with Kaunda at the helm.

This marked the apogee of the liberation struggle in present-day Zambia. Justifiably or unjustifiably, in 1972, Kaunda declared UNIP the only party thus making the country a one-party-state and also a one-party government. Zambia's adoption of the one-party constitution in 1972 could be regarded as "an attempt to create an institutional structure capable of constraining certain types of conflict and competition which had affected the stability of the political system" (Wanyande, 1995: 73). This one-party system continued until 1990 when the formation of political parties became legal in Zambia. There had been calls for democracy since 1981, but, Kaunda tried all in his power to delay the process of bringing about change. Eventually he conceded defeat and accepted the majority view. When political parties were allowed in the country there was also a need to change the National Constitution to be in line with the new political dispensation. Through all these political developments the country's political life was reconfigured quite significantly and Zambia began a new path which was characterized by optimism. Some of these points are expounded below.

5.3 Zambian Politics From 1964-2001

A point has been made that Zambia is one of the African countries that achieved independence during the first wave in the 1960s. As discussed earlier, Kaunda became the first president when the county achieved political independence in 1964. After spending more than 20 years in office, Kaunda found himself under immense pressure to relinquish power. In 1968, he banned all political parties and tried all in his power to stall the process aimed at re-introducing multi-party politics. He even toyed with the idea of holding a referendum on the issue as a way of buying time. In November 1990, Kaunda invited other Heads of States to join him and his government in a breakfast prayer in order to win religious groups. However, these tactics were bound to fail due to a number of reasons. First, during the 1980s, the standard of living of most Zambians fell due to rising unemployment (especially in the mining sector), falling real wages and the collapse of social services. Subsequently, there were illegal strikes in the public sector in the years 1985, 1987, 1988 and 1989. Food riots were also reported in 1986 and 1990 (Nugent, 2004). The Zambian Congress of Trade Unions (ZCTU) put the blame squarely at the doorstep of Kaunda's UNIP. Moreover, Zambian mainstream churches joined the fray and became openly critical of Kaunda's government. Responding to pressure, Kaunda formed the National Interim Committee for Multiparty Democracy which was tasked to accelerate the process of bringing about the desired political change. Unfortunately for him, in 1991, this Committee transformed itself into a political party, the MMD and vowed to challenge UNIP.

Following the drafting of the new National Constitution in 1990 which allowed political parties to operate in the country, the MMD and other political parties emerged. The MMD was led by Frederick Chiluba, a well know trade unionist. Chiluba began with the campaigns aimed at challenging Kaunda in the next election. UNIP's vote-buying and scare tactics did not work for Kaunda. Consequently, as fate would have it, on 2 November, 1991, Chiluba, who used the MMD ticket to contest the election, emerged victorious and thus ousted President Kaunda. He became the only second president of an independent Zambia since 1964. When the results were announced, the MMD was said to have won a total of 125 of the 150 legislative seats and Chiluba got 76% of the presidential election votes overall Kaunda conceded defeat and vacated office (Mngomezulu, 2008; Nugent, 2004). To some, this came as a great shock. However, the point worth noting is that Chiluba was a unionist and this counted on his favour because he was closer to the working class than the president who was said to be living a lavish lifestyle while the poor were suffering. Secondly, Kaunda had already ruled Zambia for almost three decades. The electorate questioned the wisdom in re-electing him to rule them again under the new political order. In the end, the majority voted against him thereby paving the way for Chiluba to hold the reigns.

But Chiluba remained suspicious of Kaunda; he feared that the latter might come back in the next election to re-claim his position as the country's president. To avert this potential situation Chiluba used state institutions and incumbency to spread lies about Kaunda and the

UNIP. In 1993 Chiluba's government claimed that UNIP was plotting a coup against his government. In response to this rumour he imposed the State of Emergency. Secondly, he put Kaunda's national identity under scrutiny, arguing that he was actually not a true Zambian because both his parents were from Malawi and not from Zambia. He contemplated deporting him to Malawi but the masses opposed this move. These efforts were meant to discredit Kaunda and dissuade some of the electorate from supporting him, should he run for the presidency again in the next election. In retrospect, it would be justifiable to say that Chiluba's tactics of sustaining his stay in power worked - at least for the time being.

Another strategy which was used by Chiluba was to remind Zambians that Kaunda had been in office for almost three decades and that he had to give other Zambians a chance to lead the country in a different style of leadership from the one he had used for so many years but which left many Zambians suffering. Chiluba "saw himself as the first in a new breed of African leaders and was determined to prove to the world that Africans were starting to take responsibility to their own affairs" (Russell, 1999: 56). He worked studiously and was also very careful with his diction. He promised Zambians a better life under his presidency where everyone would benefit. It was with these and many other promises that Chiluba won the historic general elections held in 1991.

But what is important for this discussion is not just the fact that Chiluba defeated Kaunda in a general election - important as that point might be. Instead, it is the fact that in spite of his pre-election promises, he later reneged in his promise and felt uncomfortable in his office. Before the 1996 elections, Chiluba, orchastrated the amendment of constitution which required that a Presidential Candidate must have both parents born in Zambia. This kept Kaunda out of contention for the presidency in future. In response to this action, UNIP and other opposition parties boycotted the 1996 elections. The international community was not impressed by these events and thus refused to send election observers to the country to monitor the elections as was the norm in any African election. Worse still, three of the four Internal Monitoring Bodies concluded that the 1996 elections were not free and fair. Thus, at the end of the 1996 elections, "democracy was barely surviving, and its future did not look promising" (Bratton & Posner, 1999:403). But this did not deter

Chiluba from ruling the country for the second term - something he had wished for.

Being mindful of the manner in which he had won the 1996 elections Chiluba immediately resorted to force in order to silence opposition and potential contenders for the presidency. In 1997 he imposed the second State of Emergency, arguing that UNIP was plotting a coup - an accusation which was never verified. In 1999 the Zambian High Court ruled that indeed Kaunda was not a Zambian citizen. Chiluba welcomed the ruling with a sigh of relief. But members of his own party were not impressed by his actions, including his plan to change the constitution so that it would allow him to run for the presidency for the third term when his official second term expired. They became vocal about this. In response, Chiluba expelled his Vice-President, Christon Tembo, and went on to expel eight other Cabinet Ministers during the first half of 2001. The disgruntled party members formed their own party, the Forum for Democracy and Development (FDD).

By this time it was already clear that after serving his two terms in office, Chiluba was so obsessed with power that he did not contemplate leaving office when his constitutional term ended in 2001. He had tasted power and knew the privileges that came with the presidency. This came as a shock to many Zambians - including his supporters and his former union members. It was in a bid to keep his position as president that Chiluba, like Moi, Mugabe, and others started lobbying to change the National Constitution so that he could run for the presidency for the third time and thus prolong his stay in office. This was an irony. The very person who vowed to open a new page in Zambian politics was now carving a plan to remain president beyond his constitutional mandate.

What Chiluba failed to realize was the fact that he had told the electorate before assuming office in 1991 that it was wrong for a leader to remain president indefinitely as this has many temptations and is not good for the country and the continent. He openly criticized Kaunda of having done this. Therefore, Zambians - including members of his own party - could not agree with his plan to change the National Constitution to advance his evident narcissistic political agenda. Therefore, Chiluba's plan was thwarted. In fact, the 1997 failed coup was a signal that some Zambians no longer wanted him to continue to be their President. Sentencing fifty-nine soldiers to death in 1999 for treason following the 1997 incident and their role in it did not earn Chiluba support either. It was therefore a foregone conclusion that he could no longer prolong his stay in power through the right channels. Lately, even his scare tactics did not reap any positive results for him. Thus, the curtain gradually closed down on him.

Realising that his exit from office was inevitable, Chiluba started planning to ease himself out. In this regard, he put his weight behind Levy Mwanawasa and presented him to the electorate as the right person to take the country forward. He wanted to use the latter politician as his protégé and thus ensure his soft landing when he reluctantly relinquished political power. Little did he know that by the time he took this decision to vacate office his political image had already been tainted and many Zambians had already lost confidence in him as a credible political leader. In fact, a closer analysis of this event leads to the conclusion that such a decision was ironic. Mwanawasa had resigned as Vive-President in 1994 blaming Chiluba's government of corruption (Nugent, 2004). For some reason, Chiluba thought that Mwanawasa would now protect him from possible prosecution simply because he had paved the way for him to become president. The writing was already on the wall that this was never going to be the case as Chiluba anticipated. The Zambian masses had negative perceptions about Chiluba, seeing him as treacherous and cunning. He had pleaded with the electorate to give him a chance to demonstrate what good leadership meant. After getting this mandate, he allowed his selfish interests to prevail over his unionism and nationalism - let alone his Christian beliefs. It was for this reason that even his Cabinet Ministers vowed to distance themselves from him, thus leaving him in the lurch.

In this context, the next elections in Zambia took place without Chiluba as one of the Presidential Candidates - something that did not please him. When the election results of the 2001 elections were announced, Mwanawasa emerged victorious. He won 29% of the votes while Anderson Mazoka of the United Party for National Development (UPND) obtained 27%. Former Vice-president Tembo obtained 13% of the votes. Mwanawasa was subsequently sworn in as the new president on 2 January, 2002.

5.4 President Mwanawasa: an Untamed Protégé

Given Mwanawasa's resolve to fight corruption, there was no guarantee that Chiluba would not be indicted for the economic and political crimes he committed while in office. Although Mwanawasa had been openly backed up by Chiluba during the build-up to the recently concluded election, he was determined to act independently as Head of State, uphold clean governance and enforces accountability - something he adhered to until his untimely death. As part of this philosophy President Mwanawasa resolved to prosecute Chiluba for two reasons: first, to give him an opportunity to clear his name if it were true that he did not commit the economic and political crimes he was accused of; and second, to set a precedent and demonstrate to Zambians that his administration would fight corruption with vigour regardless of who was involved in it. To clear his way, President Mwanawasa removed Chiluba's immunity from prosecution on charges of corruption. This brought some semblance of hope among many Zambians that at last the days of rampant corruption and maladministration were over and that the country was set to walk on a new path.

To buttress Mwanawasa's suspicions about Chiluba, on 4 May, 2007, the High Court in London found former President Chiluba guilty of stealing £23 million (more than R315 million) of public funds in a civil case brought to the court on behalf of the Zambian Attorney-General. Chiluba had deposited the money in overseas accounts using London-based law firms. The fact that he had once served as a trade union leader and therefore understood the plight of the working class did not seem to bother him once he became president. According to Justice Peter Smith, Chiluba earned $100, 000 (about R700, 000) between 1991 and 2001 when he was in power but was able to pay an exclusive boutique in Switzerland which saw him parting with $1.2 million. Moreover, he also had a global reputation as a smart and expensive dresser, wearing monogrammed shirts and suits as well as specially made shoes with high heels (Pretoria News, 2007; City Press, 2007).

The judge continued to say that Chiluba stole public funds at a time when the majority of Zambians were struggling to live on one dollar per day and thousands of people could not afford more than one meal a day. When the British judge ordered Chiluba to personally return $41 million of the $46 siphoned from the Zambian treasury during his ten-year rule, he cried foul and argued that the order "bordered on racism" (Business Day, 2007). Such a defence mechanism did nothing to protect Chiluba and Africa's image in global politics. He wanted to remain in power, not for the sake of his people as he had claimed when he ousted Kaunda, but so that he could satisfy his personal financial ambitions. He evidently subscribed to the notion of practicing 'the politics of the belly'. Therefore, former president Chiluba is indeed one of the African presidents who got obsessed with power and fell prey to the 'president for life' pandemic which is ravaging the African continent. This is how he will be remembered in history. His earlier trade unionism was overshadowed by his political avarice demonstrated in this chapter. Interestingly, Kaunda, the person he removed from power in 1991, is the one who will be remembered in a positive light. Although President Kaunda stayed in power for over two decades, unlike Chiluba, he did not steal from the state funds.

5.5 Conclusion

The brief history of Zambia presented in this chapter shows a country that has evolved over time and had to face many tribulations along the way. Of particular importance to our discussion is the manner in which the theme of this book is carried out in the narrative. While President Kaunda represents the first generation of African leaders, President Chiluba represents the second generation. It is clear from the discussion above that despite his utterances that he ousted Kaunda in order to lead Zambia on a new path, former President Chiluba is indeed one of the African leaders who were obsessed with political power and was not willing to relinquish it once he ascended to the throne. Like the other presidents discussed earlier in this book, Chiluba was prepared to change the National Constitution in order to achieve his personal goal and fulfil his political ambitions. As it later turned out, his attack on former President Kaunda had nothing to do whatsoever with clean governance. On the contrary, it had everything to do with his resolve to silence potential opposition. Similarly, his decision to fire his Vice-President and expel a total of eight Cabinet Ministers demonstrated his determination to prolong his stay in power with very limited or no opposition. In the same vein, Chiluba's resolve to have soldiers implicated in the alleged 1997 failed coup executed was yet another strategy to scare potential critics and contenders to his 'throne'. All these desperate measures were bound to hit back over time.

The Zambian case epitomizes the political image of African continent painted by some of its leaders. What is clear from this case study is that enjoying incumbency and fearing possible prosecution are some of the reasons why African leaders do not want to leave office. Also, the fact that these leaders use incumbency to amass personal wealth tempts them to refuse to leave office. Therefore, it would be fair to conclude that the reasons for these African leaders to want to stay in power longer than necessary are multi-fold. This trajectory leads to the conclusion that no single and one-shoe-fits-all solution could be found to address this pandemic which has engulfed the African continent over the years. However, this does not mean that no attempt at all should be made to try and alleviate the problem.

For example, creating positions in the AU to absorb former presidents could be an incentive for them to leave office when their terms expire. Another option would be for the UN to appoint at least some of them as envoys to represent the UN in different countries. People like former President Nelson Mandela of South Africa, former President Kufour of Ghana and former President Joachim Chissano of Mozambique are among a few real African leaders who made no attempts to prolong their stay in office. These leaders are a living testimony that it is possible to leave office and still enjoy the respect of your people and the international community. Former South African President Thabo Mbeki did not leave office gracefully but at least he is more useful to the African continent now than he was as the national president. What is commendable about him is that he did not resort to violence to prolong his stay in office when the ANC recalled him. But leaders like the late President Chiluba are a shame to the African continent. He epitomizes those leaders the continent feels ashamed of whenever their names are mentioned in international circles. We can only hope that in future more and more African leaders will try to understand what Constitutional Democracy means in real terms and start to respect their National Constitutions and refrain from making attempts to change such constitutions solely for their own individual, political and financial benefits.

References

Bratton, M. & D. N. Posner. (1999). "A first look at second elections in Africa with illustrations from Zambia", in R. Joseph (ed.), *State Conflict and Democracy in Africa*. Boulder and London: Lynne Rienner.

Business Day (2007). "Chiluba faces asset seizure", 17 May.

City Press, (2007). "UK court finds Chiluba guilty", 6 May.

Cobbing, J. (1988). "The mfecane as alibi: Thoughts on Dithakong and Mbolompo", *Journal of African History*. 29: 487-519.

Fage, J. D. (1986). *A History of Africa*. London: Hutchinson.

Grotpeter, J. J. (1998). *Historical Dictionary of Zambia*. Lanham, USA: Scarecrow Press.

Hamilton, C. (1995) (ed.). *The Mfecane Aftermath: Reconstructive Debates in Southern African History*. Johannesburg: Witwatersrand University Press.

Hamilton, C. (1998). *Terrific Majesty: The Powers of Shaka Zulu and the Limits of Historical Invention*. Cape Town: David Philip.

Harris, J. E. (1998). *Africans and their History. Second Revised Edition*. Canada: Penguin Books.

Herbert, E. W. (2002). *Twilight on the Zambezi: Late Colonialism in Central Africa*. Hampshire & New York: Palgrave.

Iliffe, J. (1995). *Africa: The History of a Continent*. Cambridge: Cambridge University Press.

Iliffe, J. (1998). *The African Poor*. Cambridge: Cambridge University Press.

Laband, J. (1997). *The Rise & Fall of the Zulu Nation*. London: Arms and Armour Press.

Macola, G. (2003). *Kingdom Of Kazembe: History and Politics in North-Eastern Zambia and Katanga to 1950*. Hamburg: Lit Verlag.

Mills, G. (2010). *Why Africa is Poor and What Africans Can Do About It*. Johannesburg: Penguin Books.

Mngomezulu, B. R. (2003). "Uganda's role in the failure of regional integration in East Africa in the 1960s and 1970s." Paper presented at the South African and Contemporary History Seminar, University of the Western Cape, South Africa, 12 August.

_____(2004a). "A Political History of Higher Education in East Africa, 1937-1970". Unpublished PhD Thesis, Rice University.

_____(2004b). "The Political Factor in Regional Integration in East Africa, 1920s-1967." Paper presented at the South African and Contemporary History Seminar, University of the Western Cape, South Africa, 28 September.

_____(2008). "Leadership crisis in Africa: Contextualising African leaders' obsession with power," in *Journal of Business and Management* Dynamics, Vol.2, December: 36-48.

_____(2009). "The economic and political foundations of regional integration in East Africa, 1924-1960". Paper presented at the ERSA Workshop, Mont Fleur, Stellenbosch, 16-18 November.

Nugent, P. (2004). *Africa since Independence*. New York: Palgrave Macmillan.

Oliver, R. & J. D. Fage. (1995). *A Short History of Africa*. New York: Penguin Books.

Omer-Cooper, J.D. (1966). *The Zulu Aftermath: A Nineteenth-Century Revolution in Bantu Africa*. London: Longmans.

Phiri, B. J. (2011). *A Political History of Zambia: From the Colonial Period to The Third Republic*. Trenton, USA: Africa World Press & Red Sea Press.

Pretoria News,(2007). "Chiluba guilty of stealing 23 million from Zambia", 5 May.

Roberts, A. (1976). *A History of Zambia*. New Edition. New York: Holmes & Meier.

Russell, A. (1999). *Big Men, Little People: The Leaders Who Defined Africa*. New York: New York University Press.

Saha, S. C. (1994). *History of the Tonga Chiefs and Their People in the Monze District of Zambia (American University Studies, Series 21: Regional Studies, Vol.12)*. New York: Peter Lang Publishing.

Walker, E. A. (1928). *A History of South Africa*. London: Longmans.

Wanyande, P. (1995). "Democracy and the one-party state: The African experience", in W. O. Oyugi & A. Gitonga (eds.). *Democratic Theory and Practice in Africa*. Nairobi: East African Educational Publishers.

Wylie, D. (2006). *Myth of Iron: Shaka in History*. Scottsville: University of KwaZulu NatalPress. http://www.Africanhistory.abo ut.com/od/Zambia/I/B1-Zambia-Timeline.htm.Accessedon 30 September 2011.

CHAPTER 6: MALAWI

The President for Life Phenomenon: It All Began Here

Marshall Tamuka Maposa & Bhekithemba Richard Mngomezulu

THE MAP OF MALAWI

6.1 Introduction

The geographical space that is today known as Malawi is among the many African countries that are landlocked but still strive for economic success despite its somewhat less fortunate geographical location. Geographically, the country is located in the southeast of Africa and shares borders with a number of African countries including: Zambia in the south, Tanzania in the northeast and Mozambique in the east, south and west. This means that for Malawi to do business using the Indian Ocean it has to first enter into negotiations with those countries that are located along the Indian Ocean, that is, Mozambique and Tanzania. The size of the country is estimated to be just over 118, 000 km^2 and has an estimated population of more than 13, 900, 000 in total. Some commentators call Malawi 'The warm heart of Africa' because of its hot weather. Before independence, this country was called Nyasaland and only adopted the new name 'Malawi' at independence. The latter name derived from 'Maravi' which was the old name used to refer to the Nyanja people who continue to exist in present-day Malawi. A detailed history of Malawi is captured in a number of sources by different scholars (Turner, 2008; Ceditor, 2005; Meredith, 2005; Nugent, 2004; Reader, 1999; Davidson, 1991, to name but a few). It is, therefore, not our intention in this chapter to discuss the pre-colonial history of Malawi in any significant detail. However, we shall present a quick synopsis in order to assist readers who might not be conversant with Malawian history in particular and African history in particular. We believe that such an approach will enable all the readers of this manuscript to follow the narrative of this chapter with relative ease.

Since its independence, Malawi has experienced a number of challenges at different moments. These include intermittent drought, political succession disturbances, allegations of corruption, and so on. But most importantly, the country has had its fair share of presidents who wanted to die in office and even tried to change the national constitution in order to realize their goal. Such inclinations resulted into political turmoil which willy-nilly culminated in widespread divisions among politicians and the political parties they represented. This chapter primarily focuses on who those presidents were and which strategies they used to prolong their stay in power. Lastly, the chapter locates the Malawian case study in the broader theme of this book which is about the 'president for life' pandemic that has come to characterise the African continent and painted it in bad light.

Before addressing succession politics in Malawi, it is imperative to first provide a very brief history of this country so as to give the background and context in which the succession debates and political manoeuvring discussed later in the chapter should be understood and interpreted readers. It is through this painstaking exercise that one can appreciate the history of Malawi and its leaders who pushed their personal agendas instead of addressing the needs of those who voted them into leadership positions in the first place.

6.2 A Concise History and Background of Malawi

The history of Malawi dates as far back as the 10th century. It was during this time that the Bantu communities came to settle in this area. The place was administered through native rule with no European or other forms of external influence. It continued like this until 1891 when Britain came to colonize the area as part of the notorious scramble for Africa. From that time on, the area was called Nyasaland by the British. In 1944, the locals established Nyasaland African Congress (NAC) with the aim of promoting local interests deliberately ignored by the British administrators who were only concerned about advancing their personal interests. This political party was bound to clash with British authorities who continued to do things their own way without considering the views and feelings of the local people. For example, in 1953 Britain decided to bring Nyasaland, southern Rhodesia (Zimbabwe) and northern Rhodesia (Zambia) together and established what it called the Central African Federation (CAF). The motivating factor behind the establishment of this body was mainly political. The thinking was that this would ease administration and ensure that British hegemony was felt in these areas. Another equally important reason was that financially the federation would save Britain some money by having one central administrative structure instead of running the three territories as separate entities. As expected, the indigenes were not happy whatsoever about this development. They protested but, Britain could not be easily moved or be swayed away from the idea of bringing them together.

In 1958, the NAC resolved to ask Dr. Hastings Kamuzu Banda to leave Ghana where he was working and return to Nyasaland to lead them. Dr. Banda accepted the invitation. On his return to the country,

Banda made his presence felt almost immediately. During the same year (1958) he, together with Kenneth Kaunda of Zambia, attended the All African People's Conference in Accra, Ghana. He came back rejuvenated following the support he and Kaunda received from President Kwame Nkrumah who had led the Gold Coast (now renamed Ghana) to independence the previous year. In March 1959, the colonial government in Nyasaland became impatient with rampant riots and other political activities propelled by Banda and his comrades. In response, it instituted the first State of Emergency in a bid to calm the untenable political situation. During this time, a total of 1300 Africans were incarcerated and no less than 51 lost their lives in the process (Nugent, 2004; Baker, 1997). Banda was subsequently put behind bars and was only released in 1960. But soon after his release he formed another political party, the Malawi Congress Party (MCP). In 1961, this party got the majority votes in the Legislative Council elections. The Conservative government in Britain allowed Nyasaland and northern Rhodesia to secede from the CAF between 1962 and 1963, which they did. This culminated in Banda becoming the first Prime Minister of Nyasaland in 1963. The CAF officially ceased to exist from 1 January 1964. On 6 June, 1964, Nyasaland obtained full independence with Dr. Banda at the helm. The new country was named Malawi as mentioned above.

As a way of consolidating his political power, President Banda enforced very rigid censorship over the media. Moreover, fearing that academics would be openly critical of his government, he suppressed academic debate at the country's national universities. To crown it all, he ensured that government informers were planted throughout the country to report those deemed to be rabble rousers. President Banda also established Malawi Young Pioneers (MYP) which literally became a paramilitary organization almost equivalent to the army and the police forces. In 1966, he made the country a one-party-state under the MCP. In 1970, he declared himself 'President-for-life', openly telling his people that no one had the right to challenge him in his position as president. This was, however, reversed a few years later when the political tide took a different direction. This point is expounded later in this chapter. The point worth noting from the discussion thus far is that President Banda was the architect of the concept: 'president for life'.

Once President Banda realized that he had a grip on power he started abusing it, creating himself enemies in the process.

Consequently, he met stiff resistance from various quarters. In March 1992, for example, Catholic churches in the country publicly read what was dubbed 'a pastoral letter'. Contained in the letter was overt criticism against social inequality, injustice executed by the national government on its own people, and unprecedented mass impoverishment which engulfed the country. Instead of addressing these concerns, Banda's government threatened to respond by brute force to the protesters. This angered even more Malawians. University students joined the fray and expressed their disapproval of the government's actions while rallying behind the Catholic Bishops who were prepared to take the bull by the horns and risk their lives in the process. In response, the government closed university campuses (Nugent, 2004; Van Donge, 1995). Chafukwa Chihana emerged as the leader of the dissidents. He led them to a meeting in Zambia. When he returned to Malawi at the conclusion of the meeting President Banda detained him immediately to dampen the spirit of his supporters. While he was behind bars Chihana's followers established the Alliance for Democracy (AFORD). Meanwhile, ex-MPC politicians formed the United Democratic Front (UDF). By all accounts, Banda was facing an unstoppable political tornado.

Early in 1993, both local and international pressure mounted on the government forced President Banda to hold a referendum against his will. His attempts to use state institutions and resources to influence the results failed. The 1993 referendum voted for a multi-party democracy. Interestingly, "as the political game threatened to run away from him, [President] Banda insisted that he was under no immediate obligation to organise elections" (Nugent, 2004: 406). This came as a surprise because the people had spoken and Banda simply did not want to listen. But this was simply the last kick of a dying horse. The writing was already on the wall that President Banda's days in the high office were numbered. Eventually he faced the reality and gave in when seeing that the country was becoming ungovernable. As his fortunes turned, he fell sick and was quickly rushed to South Africa for medical treatment. The diagnosis indicated that he had a brain tumour. While he was away members of his party (the MCP) disarmed the MYP and forced their leaders out of the country through what they called 'Operation Bwezani'. Holding democratic elections became inevitable and was the only obvious solution to the political crisis. AFORD had Chihana as their Presidential Candidate. UDF fielded Bakili Muluzi. But the latter was discredited by the fact that he had once served as Vice-President under Banda. Fortunately for him the other candidates did not have the political experience Muluzi had, having served in government before.

When the results of the first multi-party elections of 17 May, 1994, were announced, President Banda's MCP lost to Bakili Muluzi who pocketed 47% of the votes compared to 33% obtained by incumbent President Banda. Chihana's AFORD got 19.5% of the votes. The results showed a regional bias. The UDF had more support from the majority south population. The MCP was well supported in the central belts while AFORD enjoyed the support of the northerners. President Banda conceded defeat and left office. He later died of natural causes in 1997. This marked the end of the first chapter in Malawi's president for life syndrome.

President Muluzi took the reigns as the country's new President. However, because he had no clear majority, he was forced to strike a deal with AFORD and gave them Ministerial positions in return for their support. Through this arrangement he ran the country, assisted by AFORD, until the next election. President Muluzi served for two terms following his victory in the following elections held in 1999. But when he realized that his second term was coming to an end he started having second thoughts about vacating the office. He then made vain attempts to extend his stay in power by proposing a constitutional amendment. In fact, we should briskly mention that it was not only him who got obsessed with power. His government Ministers too had already started enjoying the benefits of holding the political offices and did not plan to relinquish such power and comfort anytime soon. Over all, "once UDF politicians had tasted the fruits of office, they were determined that power should not slip from their grasp" (Nugent, 2004: 407).

But as fate would have it, President Muluzi and his clique were eventually forced to leave office through the ballots. To ensure his soft landing, President Muluzi hand-picked Dr. Bingu wa Mutharika an American trained economists as his preferred successor. He preferred him for two reasons. First, thought that the latter would use his academic skills and revive the country's economy thus painting a positive picture about his President Muluzi) legacy. Second, he needed someone he could count on should a call be made for him to be prosecuted after vacating office. Indeed, Bingu wa Mutharika won the 2004 elections and thus succeeded former President Muluzi whose attempts to remain the country's president beyond his constitutional mandate were not successful. This is the chronology of events in Malawi which cover the pre-colonial, colonial, and early to mid-post-colonial periods.

Based on the foregoing background, the aim of the second part of this chapter is to demonstrate how the concept of life presidency in Malawi did not die with President Banda but outlived him and continued to show its ugly face in Malawian politics long after he was dead. In the next sub-sections we analyse the tenures of the three presidents as discussed above within the framework of historical change and continuity. While some of the issues and characteristics of Malawian politics were not isolated from the case studies discussed earlier in this book, we unabashedly argue that successive presidents in Malawi and elsewhere in postcolonial Africa willy-nilly continued to be influenced by former President Banda's policies and, principally, his life presidency tendencies which he did not hide or become apologetic about.

6.3 Understanding Change and Continuity

We employ the concept of change and continuity because President Banda's election resulted (or at least aimed to result) in a major change in the history of postcolonial Malawi. It marked the end of colonisation and the dawn of a new political dispensation in a period when the so-called "wind of change" was blowing across the African continent. In the same vein, the ascension of President Muluzi marked the end of a three-decade era of President Banda. In the context of the rest of the African continent political scientists characterise President Muluzi's victory as part of the "wave of democracy" or, in some cases, "the second liberation" because he falls under the second generation of the African leadership discussed in Chapter 1 of the present book. This helps illustrate how this can also be viewed as a period of change. It was a period of change in terms of events on the ground and also in terms of aspirations and directions of the country's citizenry in a new political dispensation which came about as a result of both endogenous and exogenous factors.

An historical understanding of the process of change helps us acknowledge that, amongst its several characteristics, change is never absolute. In fact, change is always characterised by uncertainties. But there is no 'absolute change' as vestiges of the old order usually remain discernable. This, therefore, means that change is invariably linked to continuity (Taylor, 2003). In other words, the process of change also simultaneously unfolds the process of continuity. What only varies in this case is the extent of either the change or the continuity. Based on this understanding and trajectory, the concept of life presidency, it will be argued, did not necessarily die instantly with President Banda in Malawi. In most cases, its remnants are sometimes manifested in subsequent political systems beyond the boundaries of Malawi. That is why we argued in Chapter 1 that President Banda was the first 'President for life' but not the last. It should be noted that life presidency in the case of this chapter is referred to not only as the title that President Banda assumed in 1970. In fact, while some leaders declare themselves presidents for life (such as Mobutu Sese Seko of formerly Zaire and François Duvalier of Haiti) some leaders are *de facto* life presidents by virtue of the way they conduct themselves in power (the late Colonel Muammar Gaddafi of Libya, the ousted President Hosni Mubarak of Egypt and President Robert Mugabe of Zimbabwe are prime examples). In this chapter, while President Banda did not die in office he was both a *de facto* and *de jure* life president by all measurements and standards. His reign was therefore characterised by the motivation which Young refers to as "office as the goal." This penchant to remain in office indefinitely would also characterise the tenures of President Banda's successors in Malawi and beyond. Our analysis in this chapter will follow the chronological history of Malawi as presented above. This will make it easier to follow the flow of events and establish the extent to which change and continuity wrestled for supremacy, primarily in the history of Malawi but also generally in Africa as a whole.

6.4 Dr. Hastings Banda: The President for Life

After about 42 years in the diaspora, Hastings Kamuzu Banda came back to his native country to lead the fight to end the Federation and ultimately secure the independence of Malawi. It did not take long for Banda to show signs of his obsession with hogging power. In fact, some historians argue that this was even evident before Banda came to power, particularly with the formation of the Malawi Congress Party (Brown, 2008). Within two years of becoming President, Banda had managed to have the constitution amended, in the process making Malawi a one-party state. A combination of the euphoria of independence and Banda's steadfast manipulation ensured that by

1970, he had been declared 'President for Life' of his party, the MCP. This accomplished, Banda managed to have himself declared 'President for Life' of Malawi just the following year. Much has been written about Banda's excesses as President of Malawi, and it is not within the scope of this chapter to enumerate and interrogate all of them. Instead, we simply raise a few aspects that were crucial to his preservation of his position of President for Life. These factors comprise what Chirambo (2004:147), refers to as Kamuzuism. He describes Kamuzuism in the following manner:

> In brief, Kamuzuism embodied the following ideas: that God chose Banda before he was born to become the leader of Malawi. Corollary to that, Banda was divinely appointed to lead Malawi for life. For this reason, he was made and fondly called "Wamuyaya," meaning President-for-life. Second, all people in Malawi wanted Banda only and no one else to lead Malawi. Third, anyone criticizing Banda was waging a war against the people of Malawi and implicitly, challenged what divine will had purported in making Banda the leader. In other words, whoever criticized or challenged Banda was against the people of Malawi, therefore, a traitor.

One feature of most analyses of Banda's reign regards his unpredictability which was meant to increase the kind of mysticism described in the above quotation. While on the one hand he could show a facade of a benevolent side, he could, on the other hand almost simultaneously, be a ruthless dictator. Both these sides were essential foundations of his life presidency. For example, he presented himself as a father figure of the nation who promoted unity and did not fuel ethnic division. As a result, his supporters credited him for creating a unified nation which managed to avoid the scourge of civil war when several other African countries were embroiled in bitter ethnic conflicts. Banda is quoted to have pronounced: "So far as I am concerned, there is no Yao in this country; no Lomwe; no Sena; no Chewa; no Ngoni; no Nyakyusa; no Tonga; there are only 'Malawians'. That is all" (Vail & White, 1989: 51). He earned respect because of his Western education and the elegance with which he held himself. The respect ended up bordering on a personality cult. This can be illustrated by the way, for example, songs and dresses were produced to celebrate him both as party leader and Head of State. His benevolent side can also be demonstrated by his promotion of women through projects such as *Chitukuko Cha Amai m'Malawi*. He used such publicity stunts in an effort to retain the support of the women of Malawi.

The mysticism behind Banda's life presidency was perpetuated more through the media which was under very strict state control as mentioned above. Because of such conservatism, Malawi had no television service until after President Banda had been removed from power. Control extended to all other forms of media such as radio and newspapers. Through the media, he showed only his perceived benevolence as the father of the nation who always provided food, shelter and clothing to "his people." This worked greatly to his favour as it limited the ordinary people's view to the country, and indeed the world, while also limiting their access to a mouthpiece to air their views. Therefore the Banda that the media exposed to the people was the *Ngwazi* (Conqueror of conquerors) as he became known, that becoming another of his several titles.

To achieve this, Banda, like President Moi in Kenya, surrounded himself with a clique of party members who had to resort to sycophancy to remain in favour and at least enjoy the benefits of the country. As a result, he had no vice-president at certain moments. If one was appointed, he quickly fired him as was the case with John Tembo. Rather, Banda worked closely with Tembo for most of his tenure. This clique was "centred on his close relatives and clients from his ethno-regional group and funded through his personal domination of the export-oriented agricultural economy" (Nasong'o, 2008). This was characteristic of the "big-man, small-boy syndrome" whereby subordinates almost worship the super-ordinate and would not dare question his decisions, let alone consider voicing against his continued tenure, no matter how convinced they were that this was politically wrong. As a result, Malawi under Banda was not just a one-party state, but sometimes it has been called a "one-man state." The 'President for Life' controlled all state apparatus such that the tentacles of his dictatorship permeated to the smallest units of the country. The assumption was that everyone was a member of the MCP and carrying around the party card was a way to avoid harassment and potential political opposition which would challenge his leadership style.

The scenario that existed for most of Banda's reign was that of forced peace and conformity. The ruthless side of Banda was especially evident in the 1970s and 1980s which Chirwa (2001), describes as "the peak of Banda's autocratic rule [which was] characterized by political detentions, deportations, and in some extreme cases, the killing of those who did not follow his political style." Part of the explanation to the prevalence of conformity was the Malawi Young Pioneers (MYP), the paramilitary wing of the MCP, which did most of the dirty work at local level to help in keeping Malawi under authoritarian control thus sustaining Banda's presidency. His political purges left most of the political power concentrated amongst his Chewa allies. However, it would be wrong to credit Banda's political longevity to the Young Pioneers only. The army had strong allegiance to the president such that they also got involved in partisan politics. So strong was Banda's control over the army that, during the transition, he was able to influence them to execute "Operation Bwezani" which disarmed members of the MYP that had been involved in the torturing and silencing of opposition at grassroots level (Chirambo, 2004). Therefore Banda's centralised control of virtually all government institutions and structures was the major factor behind him being a lifelong president. Any attempt to challenge him publicly was tantamount to committing suicide.

Nevertheless, the longer his reign lasted, the more strained Banda's capacity to retain the status quo became. By the 1990s, as demonstrated above, he had no choice, but to give in. Banda is sometimes credited for stepping down (in spite of being Life President) when the wave of Second Liberation swept across Africa. Indeed, it can be argued that the transition was relatively smooth for someone who had held so much power for so long in the process creating a cohort of opportunists around him. During his trial for the death of three opponents in 1983, he even offered a statement in which he acknowledged how "systems of government are dynamic and they are bound to change in accordance with the wishes and aspirations of the people" (Ndebvu, 2011). However, it should be noted that Banda did not merely step down simply because he now realised the aspirations of his people. If so, he would not have persecuted opposition to his position for almost the entirety of his tenure. It was a combination of internal and external pressure that left him with no option but to relinquish power. Also his ill-health drained most of the energy he would have used to fight agents of change to the bitter end.

Other than internal opposition, several other factors forced Banda to give in, but these are not the focus of this section as some have already been enumerated and discussed earlier in this chapter. The factors include; a worsening economic situation following cuts on grants, donations and fiscal aid to his government. Therefore, when a group of Catholic priests publicly condemned the government for its excesses, subsequently getting local (students, and civic groups) and international support, Banda had few options but to agree, albeit grudgingly, to a referendum for multiparty democracy (Ihonvbere, 1997). This decision should not only be interpreted as Banda's realisation that the end was nigh. It should also not be misconstrued as reminiscent of his repentance. Banda was far from that. In fact, he did not expect to lose the referendum, considering the way he had had the citizens of Malawi under his sound control, to the point of taking them for granted. Also, he believed that his incumbency and his access to state institutions and resources would enable him to swing the results the way he wanted. In retrospect, this proved to be a miscalculation on his part. He underestimated his people and thereby shot himself on the foot as it were.

The mere fact that Malawi had to go through a referendum for Banda to realise that the general populace did not support his life presidency demonstrates his delusion while basking in the glory of power. Furthermore, the fact that the MCP even went on to field Banda (already in his nineties) in the following multiparty elections - even despite the fact that 63.5% of the voters had rejected one-party politics - also serves to confirm the delusional self-belief, if not outright desperation, that Banda and his MCP had at the time. Alternatively, potential presidential candidates from the MCP might have been reluctant to come forth to stand for the election fearing that he still had some power and influence he would revert to in order to make their lives hell for challenging him. Those who held such thoughts can be pardoned. A tin that once contained poison will still read "poisonous" long after the poison had been washed away by rain and made ineffective by other natural elements. He had wielded power for too long and they had a reason to fear him.

What the above means is that, Banda, like most leaders who had multiparty elections after a long time, was taken by surprise by the turn of events and suddenly found himself too weak to try and turn the tide in an instant. Still, despite having control of the media, violence on opponents by the MYP and other factors linked to his advantageous incumbency, Banda still lost the 1994 election fairly and squarely to a fractured opposition. Thus ended the reign of Malawi's 'President for Life', soon to die three years later, but his protracted time would influence the country's politics long after he was gone. As Daniel arap Moi once stated in Kenya, one learns from the main architects.

Kenyatta had taught Moi how to play the ethnicity card. When he assumed power, Moi did the same. In Malawi too, those who watched Banda's leadership tactics learnt from him and thus felt comfortable to use a similar language and skills to prolong their stay in power when it was their turn.

6.5 Bakili Muluzi: Old Wine in New Skins?

As discussed earlier in this chapter, the first multiparty elections in Malawi were held in 1994 following the results of the referendum. The winner of the presidential election was Bakili Muluzi, leader of the United Democratic Front with 1.4 million (47%) votes, while Banda came second with 996 363 (33%) votes (Ihonvbere, 1997:237). The expectations on Muluzi's shoulders were enormous and he had to prove to his detractors that change had indeed eventually come to Malawi, by not showing Banda's characteristics. After all Muluzi had once been part of Banda's party and government before falling out of favour with the 'President for Life'. In the end, Muluzi did not do much to convince the Malawi citizenry that he was indeed a departure from Banda and the MCP. Therefore, although Muluzi won re-election for a second term in 1999 against a joint MCP-AFORD candidate, Gwandaguluwe Chakuamba, his support had diminished considerably compared to what it had been in the 1994 election. In fact, the 1999 election was marred by controversy which the electoral commission never adequately nor convincingly addressed for reasons yet to be satisfactorily enumerated and discussed.

It would be an exaggeration to label Muluzi a dictator in the Banda sense. He did introduce a number of liberties. Most importantly, political parties mushroomed and there was no major retribution on past offenders as some had anticipated. An attempt was made to heal the wounds of the past by establishing a Truth Commission which heard cases of the previous government's abuses. A number of victims received some compensation, although the transparency of the process was questioned when it emerged that it was mostly those in government who were benefiting. However, democracy is not just about changing faces, but is also building institutions that offer long lasting protection to the will of the people. Therefore, Malawi, coming from a personal dictatorship, struggled in this aspect no matter how hard the new leadership tried to do things differently.

One of the earliest signs of Muluzi's attempts to have unlimited power concerned the senate debacle. Civic society had pushed for the establishment of a Senate, a second chamber which would serve to limit whatever excesses the parliament would want to excuse. Muluzi did not favour the establishment of a Senate. He did not point out the real reason why he objected, but hid behind the argument that Malawi could not afford to run two chambers. This argument baffled many and Ihonvbere (1997: 241), expressed the paradox that, in spite of Muluzi's claim of financial constraints, he still had "a large cabinet, with many irrelevant ministerial appointments. More importantly, it was strange that a price was being put on democracy, checks and balances and the containment of tyranny." Following long deliberation at the constitutional conference of 1995, Muluzi announced that the Senate chamber would be introduced in 1999. For political analysts, this was just a gimmick which Muluzi would use to avoid defeat in the 1999 election. In other words, had there been no plan to hold elections in 1999, the Senate proposal would have been rejected outright. Still, by the time of the 1999 election, Muluzi had managed to have the senate constitutional provision abolished therefore allaying worries about reduction of his executive powers. Whatever promises he made amounted to nothing beyond simply buying time while he ruminated about the next strategy he would employ in order to entrench his authority and sustain his stay in power.

It was in his second term of office that Muluzi's tendencies for long-term control of the country came to the surface. Like his predecessor, the more he stayed in power the more corrupt and self-serving he became. The ordinary lot, especially in the rural areas, including in the south where he got his largest vote share, remained poor. President Muluzi began to dismantle the institutions that he had initially tried, or at least pretended, to build. It is the observation of Nasong'o (2008) that, "for most of Muluzi's presidency, there was a systematic weakening of all institutions of accountability." The "big-man, small-boy syndrome" began to creep in again. It now seemed as if Muluzi's clique had only fought to get their chance on the gravy train. In the process, President Muluzi seemed to rely on reference to Banda's dictatorship whenever he wanted to validate himself as a democrat. In reality, though, the remnants of Banda's philosophy were evident as a personality cult began to grow around him.

Similar to the case of Banda's time, the media was an important tool for President Muluzi's control of information. It should however, be acknowledged that, in comparison to Banda, Muluzi had liberalized information a bit more. In addition, he had overseen the establishment of television broadcast in the country. But, television became his baby as he seemed to feel entitled to it because he had made it possible. In fact, President Muluzi's party made no secret of that fact as was declared by Joseph Kubwalo, the Minister of defence and UDF campaign director who was quoted by Nasong'o (2008) to have said, "It was him [Muluzi] who started it and he has all the right to make use of the television." The culture of self-entitlement and sycophancy was back. Comparing President Muluzi to former President Banda, Chirwa (2001:23) noted that:

> As was the case during Banda's presidency, wherever Bakili Muluzi, the current president, goes, there is always a coterie of women dressed in yellow, his party's official colour, dancing, ululating, and singing praises to him and his party. The songs are full of mockery, hate mongering, character assassination and condemnation of the previous regime and its key officials.

When it came to media coverage, for the ordinary citizen, the remnants of former President Banda were clear to see even during President Muluzi's first term of office (Ihonvbere, 1997). The system of patronage meant that the democratization of Malawi became a mirage. Included in the system were the Young Democrats, youths of the UDF, who got favours by harassing ordinary members of society and cowing them into silence or supporting their party. While the abuses of the Young Democrats cannot be equated in measure to those perpetrated by Banda's MYPs, President Muluzi had adopted Banda's tactics of getting support through spreading fear. Some of the Young Democrats were even said to be former members of the MYP and therefore knew the benefits of torturing the citizenry. Although President Muluzi distanced himself from any of their violence, Lwanda (2006:543) contends that the Young Democrats were, in fact, paid "to administer physical violence." This is a difficult assertion to refute if one looks at issues in the broader light.

During his second term in office, President Muluzi then went on to demonstrate the ultimate of Banda's tendencies: "office as the goal." He embarked on a quest to extend his tenure by trying to get a third term in office. However, civic society and opposition parties did not take this lightly and the matter ended in the court. Again, President Muluzi was showing delusions by thinking that the court would declare him eligible. In any case, there had been a history of him meddling with the judiciary, an institution that is supposed to be independent in any democratic setting. For example, in 2001 Justice Mwaungulu and two other senior judges came under fire as UDF members of parliament moved a motion to impeach them for favouring the opposition. Debates on the constitutional amendment had resulted in scuffles, both inside and outside parliament (*IRIN*, 28 January, 2003).

As opponents realized that President Muluzi was turning into another 'life president' demonstrations broke out. Like in the old days under Banda, the government quickly responded by summarily banning them. Despite a court ruling allowing the demonstrations to go ahead, President Muluzi threatened to use force to quash them. It is then that the term dictator began to be thrown around to describe his political system. He denied any dictatorial tendencies, but claimed that he wouldn't mind being called so as long as he maintained peace and stability in the country (*Mail & Guardian*, 2003). This takes us back to Banda being proud of Malawi not having civil strife when, in fact, the supposed peace was forced peace on the citizenry, an antithesis of democratic practice.

President Muluzi's attempts to get a third term were roundly rejected. In the end, he had to make do with retaining his position as leader of the UDF and then handpicking Bingu wa Mutharika to become his successor - the same strategy employed by President Moi in Kenya, President Chiluba in Zambia and President Obasanjo in Nigeria. This was in the hope that Mutharika would secure his worries and his influence would still be felt from his position as ruling party leader. It was the same strategy used by Moi when he handpicked Uhuru Kenyatta, Obasanjo when he handpicked Alhaji Umaru Yar'Adua and Chiluba when he handpicked Levy Mwanawasa. For President Muluzi, the plan did not work perfectly though. Mutharika won the 2004 elections, but he was not prepared to play second fiddle when he was President of the country, the same way that Mwanawasa did in Zambia. This left Muluzi in the cold, but Malawi had managed to get rid of a purveyor of the remnants of Banda's political philosophies.

However, it should be noted that Muluzi's penchant for power did not die in 2004. Even in 2011, there was still talk of Muluzi wanting to come back and run for a third term after lying low for some time to allow himself a chance to study the direction the political tide was moving towards. This is after the constitutional court again had to make a ruling, barring him from making a presidential comeback. Muluzi's cogently coined argument was that the term limits only applied to two consecutive terms and did not refer to someone who had left office and only came back to contest the election at a later date (*IOL*, 2009). After failing in all these avenues, the only chance that remained for Muluzi to influence Malawian politics was if his son, Atupele, were to win party presidency for a start. This idea of grooming sons to represent their fathers is becoming a menace in African politics. This was the case, for example, with President Hosni Mubarak in Egypt and Colonel Muammar Gaddafi in Libya, among others.

6.6 Bingu Wa Mutharika: Learning From The Predecessor

As the anointed successor, Mutharika managed to defeat Chakuamba in the 2004 election by a ten point margin. He rode the excesses of the Young Democrats in the hotly contested election. His being handpicked by Muluzi did not do him much favours, but he seemed to get the public on his side in 2005 when he ditched Muluzi by quitting the UDF, forming his own party, the Democratic Progressive Party (DPP), and hauling Muluzi to the courts for corruption. The new party attracted members from the wide spectrum of Malawian political parties. For example, in 2006, ex-leader Hastings Banda's nephew, Ken Kandodo, a senior member of the MCP, joined the DPP and got a cabinet post as Finance Minister. This incident surprised many who did not see it coming.

Although the new politicians were not entirely new on the political scene, they seemed to offer something different with a hope of moving farther away from the autocracy of Banda. There was evident economic growth and the government claimed success with its national seed and fertiliser programme which ran every year until the next election. For once, the country became self-sufficient in terms of food supply. In the 2009 election, the majority (55%) chose to re-elect President Mutharika at the expense of Banda's strongman, John Tembo of the MCP. Even the present-day detractors of Mutharika agree that, "Mutharika wasn't a bad president, in his first term at least" (Allison, 2011).

But Mutharika's second term has not been that rosy though. His success in re-election after forming his own party gave him a touch of arrogance. His star also rose on the continent as he led the African Union. Suddenly he assumed, in some quarters, Banda's old title, *Ngwazi*, in full being referred to as President Ngwazi Professor Bingu wa Mutharika (Allison, 2011). Amidst such pomp, talk of aiming for a third term started once again. In fact, some members of the DPP publicly spelt out that Mutharika should get a third term. This did not seem to gain popular support, but in 2009, DPP parliamentarians, Nsanje North MP Frank Viyaji moved the motion that the presidential term be increased from five to seven years, and proposed that it be taken to parliament (Cammack, 2009). That they saw nothing wrong with the motion can be taken to be evidence of the conditioning of some sections of the citizenry by Banda's life presidency. Mutharika himself dispelled any thoughts of him going for a third term. This came as relief to those Malawians who still believed in embracing democratic practices.

As of 2011, the talk of a third term had not died down. The latest person to refute the claims was the Presidential Spokesperson Hetherwick Ntaba (Liabuba, 2011). It should be worrying for those against life presidency that there was even talk of extending presidential tenures, whether it was being dispelled or not. Mutharika might have given up on a third term, but another development, similar to what happened between him and Muluzi remained on the cards. Mutharika handpicked his successor, but his option seemed to be safer. In August 2011, the DPP Secretary General Wakuda Kamanga announced in confident fashion: "Malawi's ruling Democratic Progressive Party (DPP) combed, screened, and searched all its rank and file and found out that the only capable person to lead the party in 2014 elections is Professor Peter Mutharika" (Chiumia, 2011). Peter Mutharika happened to be the incumbent's brother. Interestingly Kamanga had just been elevated to position of Secretary General after Binton Kutsaira was fired and no clear reasons were made public (Zulu, 2011). Some ruling party officials made no secret of the fact that they preferred Peter Mutharika because he was related to the outgoing president (Allison, 2011). What this means to African politics remains a point for further debate. Unfortunately time and space will not allow us to expound this point.

Such developments served to increase a state of uneasiness in Malawi, as President Mutharika was viewed to be trying to retain control of the country through the back door. President Mutharika's major test was his response to the demonstrations and riots that gripped the country in mid-2011. Some reports claimed that: "the DPP youth brandished machetes in the streets of Blantyre to instil fear into Malawians who wanted to demonstrate against Mutharika's poor political and economic governance" (Zulu, 2011). Evidently, Mutharika's party inherited a culture of violent youth wings after the MYP of Banda and the Young Democrats of Muluzi. This shows how the country has continued struggling to shake off the remnants of Banda's life presidency. It is in this context that we argue that despite some changes in Malawian history after the death of President Banda, vestiges of the old order remain. Change and continuity still wrestle for supremacy. The success of each will determine the future of Malawi and, by extension, that of the African continent as a whole.

6.7 Conclusion

Malawi has now gone over half a century of independence from colonial Britain. However, the citizens are yet to fully enjoy the benefits of this independence they yearned for. As demonstrated in the discussion above, the county was plunged into three decades of dictatorship under President Kamuzu Banda who declared himself 'President for Life' and used brute force to sustain himself and his government against the wishes of the people. Sadly, long after his death, Banda's influence is still evident in the country. His successor, President Bakili Muluzi, disappointed the electorate by almost entirely following the same way as Banda. The successive President, Bingu wa Mutharika, started with a lot of promise for the country. However, his dedication to democracy was being put under the test as the country went through political and economic problems. For a moment, at least, he seemed to be learning fast from Muluzi's book. It was a matter of new wine in old skins. Those who look at Malawi's political history from a distance do not see any major deviation from the practices of the country's founding president, Kamuzu Banda.

This chapter has traced the history of Malawi through the pre-colonial, colonial and post-colonial times. It has, in particular, discussed the presidency of the three consecutive presidents, that is, Presidents Banda, Muluzi and Mutharika. Most importantly, the chapter has drawn similarities and differences between Malawian history and the histories of the other case studies discussed in this manuscript. What seems similar is the fact that in Malawi, as in the other case studies, there is evidence of deliberate attempts by sitting presidents to prolong their stay in office. To do this, they reverted to the use of the carrot and stick approach. This strategy played itself out in the sense that those who were greedy could be bought easily by the sitting president. However, those who appeared to be principled or simply did not like the incumbent president were persecuted, incarcerated, and, in worse case scenarios assassinated. What is clear in this and the previous chapters is that having access to state institutions and resources, political leaders do all in their power to occupy leadership positions beyond their constitutional mandate. What seems to differ, as discussed in this chapter, is the extent to which obsession with power manifests itself, but the intention remains the same. The continued existence of this practice on the African continent is a serious concern, not only for Malawi as a country, but for Africa as a whole. In the case of Malawi, we can only hope that the current president, Joyce Banda, will open a new page in Malawi's history. The fact that she voluntarily cut down her salary to set an example is a positive gesture which paints an optimistic picture about Malawi.

References

Allison, S. (2011). President Mutharika, the man who's overstayed Malawi's hospitality. *The Daily Maverick.*

Baker, C. (1997). *State of Emergency: Crisis in Central Africa, Nyasaland, 1959-1960.* London and New York: Taurus.

Cammack, D. (2009). Ruling DPP to extend Mutharika's term limit in office. *Governance in Malawi, Past and Future.* Institute of Development Studies.

Ceditor, M. P. (2005). *Central Africa: Close Association 1945-1958.* London: The Stationary Office.

Chirambo, R. (2004). "Operation Bwezani": the army, political change, and Dr. Banda's hegemony in Malawi. *Nordic Journal of African Studies* 13(2) 146–163.

Chirwa, W.C. (2001). Dancing towards dictatorship: Political songs and popular culture in Malawi. *Nordic Journal of African Studies* 10(1) 1-27.

Davidson, B. (1991). *African History: Themes and Outlines. Revised and Expanded Edition.* New York: Collier Books & Macmillan Publishing.

IOL, (2009). Court to rule on Muluzi third term bid.

Ihonvbere, J.O. (1997). From despotism to democracy: The rise of multiparty politics in Malawi. Third World Quarterly, 18(2) 225-247.Retrieved 26 August 2011from, http://www.jstor.org/stable/39 93221.

IRIN (2003). Scuffles delay decision on Muluzi third term.

Liabuba, D. (2011). No third term for Mutharika.

Meredith, M. (2005). *The Fate of Africa – From the Hopes of Freedom to the Heart of Despair: A History of 50 Years of Independence.* New York: Public Affairs.

Nasong'o, S.W. (2008). The transition from a personal dictatorship: Democratization and the legacy of the past in Malawi. *The African Search for Stable Forms of Statehood: Essays in Political Criticism.* Lewiston: Edwin Mellen Press. 187-227.

Ndebvu, H. (2011). Why Malawi should celebrate Kamuzu Banda.

Nugent, P. (2004). *Africa since Independence.* New York: Palgrave Macmillan.

Lwanda, J. (2006). "Kwacha: The violence of money in Malawi's politics, 1954-2004". *Journal of Southern African Studies*, 32(3) 525-544. Retrieved 26 August 2011from http://www.jstor.org/stabl e/25065121.

Mail & Guardian (2003). "Malawi bars demos against Muluzi's third term bid."

Reader, J. (1999). *Africa: A Biography of the Continent.* New York: Vintage Books.

Taylor, T. (2003). *Historical Literacy: Making History: A Guide for the Teaching and Learning of History in Australian Schools.* Australia: Curriculum Corporation.

Turner, B. (2008). (ed.) *The Statesman's Year Book 2009: The Politics, Culture and Economies of the World.* New York: Macmillan Publishers.

Vail, L & White, L. (1989). Tribalism in the Political History of Malawi.

Van Donge, J. K. (1995). "Kamuzu's legacy: The democratisation of Malawi", *African Affairs*, 94 (375): 230.

Zulu, K. (2011). DPP fires Secretary General and endorses Peter Mutharika for 2014. *Malawi Today.*

OVERALL CONCLUSION: GAMBLING WITH THE CONTINENT'S FUTURE

Bhekithemba Richard Mngomezulu

One of the realities of African history is that it has been characterized by blatant distortions and misrepresentations derived from a wide range of causal factors. These factors range from using wrong sources, disregarding oral sources and dismissing African methods of preserving history as primitive, obsolete and outmoded. Before the advent of colonialism, African communities in their various geographical spaces had an accurate safeguarding of their local histories. They did this through oral narratives and by making the use of griots and praise singers (*izimbongi*). Some of the innovations used by African communities to preserve their histories included but were not necessarily limited to: folktales, fairy tales, legends, fables and myths. Similarly, the common usage of idioms and proverbs in people's everyday life supplemented these forms of preserving societal histories. Novels written by African scholars such as the Nigerian prolific writer, Chinua Achebe, the Kenyan novelist Ngugi wa Thiong'o, the Somalian, Nurudin Farah and many others capture the African pasts elegantly. In their writing, the authors mentioned here use their novel writing skills to make African histories easily accessible to a wider audience and not just those interested in African history as an academic field. From the works of African scholars like the ones enumerated above, we learn that as African children grew up they were both directly and indirectly taught about the histories of their communities and were, therefore, introduced to the African repertoire and were also taught about social taboos.

One of the sad realities of colonialism and Christianity is that they both discouraged the afore-mentioned forms of history preservation. As much as the missionaries taught Africans how to read and write-something from which a number of African scholars benefited - the reality is that, by and large, missionaries did not encourage African children to appreciate their histories. The primary reason why missionaries taught African children was to enable them to read the Bible and thus assist the missionaries in their evangelization work in Africa. As for the colonial state, the main interest of its representatives was to train young Africans who would assist colonial authorities in the administration of the colonies. This created fertile ground for and perpetuated indirect rule (Mamdani, 1996). It is for this reason that young Africans were not encouraged to further their education. The reason why African higher education received attention at a later period was political. In the case of East Africa, for example, Britain supported the idea of promoting higher education in the region in order to avert potential political agitation by young East Africans who studied abroad. The thinking was that African students who studied in Europe and at the Tuskegee Institute in America were exposed to political ideas and created a number of problems for the colonial state when they returned to East Africa from abroad after completing their studies (Mngomezulu, 2012; Mngomezulu, 2010; Mngomezulu, 2004; Kelley & Lewis, 2000; King, 1971).

The dawn of democracy in Africa from the 1960s onwards brought a glimmer of hope that the African continent was on the right course. Indeed, in the academic field this seemed to be the case. African scholars embarked on an intense project of re-writing African histories to debunk the myths created and perpetuated by mostly Western scholars. These African intellectuals produced local histories of specific communities in the 1960s and 1970s (Ogot, 1967a; Ogot, 1967b; Ogot, 1964). This project continued in the 1980s and 1990s (Atieno Odhiambo & Cohen, 1989; Bhabha, 1994; Cohen & Atieno Odhiambo, 1987; Fairhead & Melisa, 1996; Kanogo, 1987; Kusimba, 1999; Ogot, B. A. & Ochieng, W. R., 1995).

In the political sphere, nationalist leaders came out of the bushes from where they had been fighting white colonialists and took charge of African affairs as Heads of States. Thus, the euphoria of independence was characterized by optimism, pride and passion. For most African countries this hope for a better future seemed not to be misplaced. A semblance of order prevailed as former guerrillas abandoned their arms and resumed the civilian lifestyle. The new political leaders promised the masses a better life devoid of past oppression by the white interlopers. This was the Africa envisioned by the freedom fighters who engaged colonial forces and fought to the bitter end. As a form of reward, some of those who had been at the vanguard of the liberation struggle were voted into power and tasked to take African nations forward.

But as this book has demonstrated, a number of African leaders reneged on their promises. Once they assumed positions of power and started enjoying the luxuries that came with incumbency, they became obsessed with power and relished the wealth which accrued to them. They did not envision a situation whereby they would let it slip away and fall on other hands. To ensure that this goal was achieved, most African leaders opted for one-party governments. This was the case in countries such as Zambia, Kenya, Tanzania and many others. Being mindful of the fact that the spirit of nationalism was at its peak, African leaders consolidated their positions under the guise of uniting their nations under one political party. Presenting themselves as true African leaders, some invented new systems of African philosophy. This was epitomized by President Nyerere's *ujamaa* in Tanzania and President Kaunda's *humanism* in Zambia.

On the side-line however, some African leaders carved plans to prolong their stay in office, disregarding the will of the people. Noticeably, some of the national constitutions did not prescribe the maximum number of years a leader could remain in power. Worse still, most of these constitutions gave immunity to prosecution to an incumbent president. Thus, the first generation of African leaders managed to prolong their stay in power, operating within the confines of the law. Some of them, together with the second generation of leaders, prolonged their stay in office partly by literally buying support, but also through the use of brute force and intimidation. The masses let them do this not because they liked the practice, but because they feared that they might be killed by the very people they considered to be their protectors. This was an unfortunate situation for the African continent which had languished in European subordination for several decades before obtaining the hard-fought independence.

Sadly, the bad practice by African leaders of holding on to power indefinitely has continued unabated to-date. In 2012, the 85-year old President Abdulaye Wade of Senegal expressed an interest to run for the presidency for the third time. Like in the cases discussed above, he was prepared to amend the national constitution in order to achieve this goal. In Zimbabwe, President Mugabe celebrated his 89th birthday in 2013 but unabashedly announced that he still wanted to run for the presidency despite having been in that position since 1980 as Prime Minister and since 1987 as executive president. The list goes on.

The five case studies discussed in this book are not the only ones on the African continent. These have been selected simply to illustrate the theme of this manuscript. The discussion in the several chapters contained in this book leads to two conclusions. Firstly, that the first generation of African leaders enjoyed an overwhelming support of their fellow nationals who took it as a given that their leaders fought colonialism and therefore had to be rewarded for their dedication. In that sense, by and large, the first generation of African leaders received the blessings of their people. Secondly, the second generation of African leaders (and those who remained from the first generation) assumed power under false pretence. They argued that they were assuming power in order to bring about change. But once in office they created more enemies by eliminating potential political enemies and by intimidating their families and supporters. They soon realized that as long as they remained presidents they could not be prosecuted and thus opted to extend their stay in power. The strategies they used, as shown through the case studies discussed in this book, included buying support, using force, intimidation and political assassinations. All these tactics were meant to instil fear within the populace. Indeed, some succeeded in executing this plan but others failed, either in their first attempts or at a later stage in their political careers.

A question arises: To what extent did African countries embrace democracy? The cases discussed in this book invoke this question and reminds us of the late Claude Ake's title: *The feasibility of democracy in Africa* (2003). Inferred in this title is that, the African continent is a special case and that the political ground is not fertile for liberal democracy. If this view is anything to go by, one would be tempted to subscribe to it. For decades after independence most African countries lived under one-party rule. It was only in the 1990s that the wheels of democracy started to turn. But even then, the incumbent leadership used state resources to prolong their stay in office. Of course, this time they were doing it under the guise of democracy. The rigging of the elections, intimidation of the electorate and potential political contenders, as well as political assassinations continued in most African countries even under the democratic dispensation. In the same vein, ethnicity and tribalism continued to dominate the political arena in Africa, as much as religion and the north-south divide did in countries like Nigeria, Sudan, Somalia and a few others. In this sense, democracy has been compromised in Africa, to borrow Ntsebeza's (2006) title.

Now, if the remnants of the old order remain even after democracy has been embraced in Africa, what does the future hold for the continent? President Mugabe in Zimbabwe has continuously been declared the winner of the presidential elections even if evidence points to the contrary. President Joseph Kabila ruled the DRC for ten years following the assassination of his father, Laurent Kabila, but still availed himself for the presidency during the November 2011 elections, which he allegedly won. In the five cases discussed in this book, all the presidents mentioned tried to prolong their stay in office within the democratic context. Instead of using the barrel of the gun as was the case before, some made vain attempts to change the constitutions of their countries to allow them to run for the top position in the land for the third term. By so doing these African leaders were already gambling with the future of the continent and other continue to do so today. It is not clear when the democratic ethos will be deeply ingrained in the minds of African political leaders. Those who are in power do not want to relinquish it. Those still outside of the gravy train try with tenacity to ride on and even revert to undemocratic methods to satisfy their political ambitions. They justify their actions by pointing out the mistakes of the incumbent presidents. Interestingly, once they ascend to the envied leadership positions they repeat the same mistakes they were pointing out while vying for office. Frederick Chiluba, Bakili Muluzi, Olusegun Obasanjo and many others used this strategy and later reneged on their promise to deliver good governance and uphold the principles of democracy. Therefore, unless the African leadership desists from being obsessed with power in the manner they are doing, the 'president for life' pandemic will continue to dent the image of African continent and determine its political image in the international arena. The tendency by the African leadership to push the 'politics of the belly' has tainted Africa's image on the global scene. The prevalence of such tendencies put the future of the continent in limbo.

However, as hinted in the foreword of this manuscript, Africans did not invent dictatorship. History teaches us that dictatorial tendencies can be traced back to the Roman Republic where the "extraordinary magistrate" dished out instructions unopposed and was almost a law unto himself. But be that as it may, this is not an excuse that African leaders can use to justify their tendency to cling on to political positions beyond their constitutional mandate. The onus is on Africans themselves to rescue the situation and despise dictatorial tendencies.

Among the possible solutions proposed in this manuscript is that incumbent presidents should be given incentives to vacate office. They should be assured that if they run their countries democratically, serve their people well, and leave office when their terms end they would be rewarded. Such rewards could include appointing a former president to a position in the AU or making him or her a UN envoy. Others could be brought together into advisory structures where they would still serve the African continent and the world in a much bigger forum than just their respective countries. If the saying 'African solutions to African problems' is anything to go by, African leaders have a direct responsibility to live by it and put their house in order. Crying over colonialism and apartheid is now a mundane and obsolete excuse which no longer holds. As much as these historical moments ruined the lives of African people and retarded their progress in all spheres of life, Africans have been free long enough to be able to decide how they would like their future to be. Importantly, individual African leaders have a chance to decide how they would like to be remembered by future generations. Neither colonial nor apartheid legacies can prevent them from making such a decision. All that is needed is the political will to do the right thing. Giving agency to colonialism and apartheid is defeatist approach to life and will not take the African continent forward.

References

Ake, C. (2003). *The feasibility of democracy in Africa.* Dakar: CODESRIA.

Atieno Odhiambo, E. S. & Cohen, D. W. (1989). *Siaya: The historical anthropology of an African landscape.* London: James Currey.

Bhabha, H. (1994). *The location of culture.* London & New York: Routledge.

Cohen, D. W. & Atieno Odhiambo, E. S. (1987). "Ayany, Malo and Ogot: Historians in search of a Luo Nation," *Cahiers d'Etudes Africaines*: 269-286.

Ehret, C. (1998). *An East African classical age*. Charottesville: University Press of Virginia

Fairhead, J. & Melisa, L. (1996). *Misreading the African landscape: Society and ecology in a forest-savamma mosaic*. Cambridge: Cambridge University Press.

Kanogo, T. (1987). *Squatters and the roots of Mau Mau*. London: James Currey.

Kelley, R. D. G. & Lewis, E. (2000). (eds.). *To make our world anew: A history of African Americans*. USA: Oxford University Press.

King, K. J. (1971). *Pan-Africanism and education: A study of race philanthropy and education in the Southern States of America and East Africa*. Oxford: Clarendon Press.

Kusimba, C. M. (1999). *The rise and fall of Swahili states.* Walnut Creek: Altamira Press.

Mamdani, M. (1996). *Citizen and subject: Contemporary Africa and the legacy of late colonialism*. Kampala, Cape Town and London: Fountain, David Philip and James Currey.

Mngomezulu, B. R. (2004). "A political history of higher education in East Africa: The rise and fall of the University of East Africa, 1937-1970." Unpublished PhD Thesis, Rice University.

_____. (2010). "The political factor in the development of education in East Africa, 1920s-1963," *Analytical reports in International Education*, 3(1) (June): 7-32.

_____. (2012). *Politics and higher education in East Africa from the 1920s to 1970*. Bloemfontein: Sun Media.

Ntsebeza, L. (2006). *Democracy compromised: Chiefs and the politics of land in South Africa*.

Cape Town: HSRC Press.

Ogot, B. A. (1964). "Kingship and statelessness among the Nilotes," in J. Vansina, R. Mauny and L. V. Thomas (eds.) *The historian in tropical Africa*. London: Oxford University Press.

_____. (1967a). *History of the Southern Luo: Volume 1, migration and settlement*. Nairobi: East African Publishing House.

_____. (167b). "Reintroducing the African man into the world: transitionalism and socialism in African politics," *East Africa Journal*, 4, 8 (Dec.): 31-36.

INDEX

www.ingramcontent.com/pod-product-compliance
Lightning Source LLC
Chambersburg PA
CBHW061746270326
41928CB00011B/2389